D0265166

Travels with an Archaeologist

Also available from Bloomsbury

The Archaeology of Mediterranean Placemaking, Richard Hodges
Beastly Questions, Naomi Sykes
Cleopatra's Needles, Bob Brier

Travels with an Archaeologist

Finding a Sense of Place

Richard Hodges

Bloomsbury Academic
An imprint of Bloomsbury Publishing Plc

B L O O M S B U R Y
LONDON · OXFORD · NEW YORK · NEW DELHI · SYDNEY

Bloomsbury Academic

An imprint of Bloomsbury Publishing Plc

50 Bedford Square	1385 Broadway
London	New York
WC1B 3DP	NY 10018
UK	USA

www.bloomsbury.com

BLOOMSBURY and the Diana logo are trademarks of Bloomsbury Publishing Plc

First published 2017

British Library Cataloguing-in-Publication Data
A catalogue record for this book is available from the British Library.

ISBN:	HB:	978-1-3500-1264-6
	ePDF:	978-1-3500-1266-0
	ePub:	978-1-3500-1265-3

Library of Congress Cataloging-in-Publication Data
A catalog record for this book is available from the Library of Congress.

Cover image © John Mitchell

Typeset by RefineCatch Limited, Bungay, Suffolk
Printed and bound in India

To my father and the memory of my mother

Contents

List of Illustrations

Photographs are by Richard Hodges unless otherwise stated.

Preface and Acknowledgements

A fresco depicting the prophet Micah found in excavations at San Vincenzo al Volturno (courtesy John Mitchell).

I became an archaeologist to travel to the past. To begin with, as a teenage digger excavating a Roman villa in my Wiltshire village, I was simply thrilled by the physicality of the journey, of unearthing discoveries. Later, my doctoral adviser, David Peacock, counselled me, archaeology is everywhere: 'it is wonderful adventure, pursue it by studying ancient commerce'. He might have added that a good restaurant and a memorable bottle of wine were part of the experience, especially if, as in my case, the thesis involved the history of the wine trade. With time, besides the sensual physicality of discovery, I came to grasp that the thrill of travel to challenge your senses naturally accompanies a career in unearthing new narratives of the past. With travel come books – biographies, histories, memoirs, novels and poetry – all enhancing the spirit of places, discrete pleasures for each adventure. No less important are fellow archaeologists whose digs serve as surrogate homes and whose company connotes precious threads in a life of study and debate.

The essays that form these chapters are some of the many I have written about places and people, and above all their spirit. I have selected them for two reasons – those that recall the company of friends in making places, and those that in some way or another convey the senses of the past – of hearing, sight, smell, taste and touch. Most of these, published between 2005 and 2016, owe their genesis to working with the Butrint Foundation in Albania, the University of Pennsylvania Museum, and now the American University of Rome. To my patient colleagues at these three institutions I am much indebted.

All but Chapter 1 were first published as 'postcards' in *Current World Archaeology*. I am especially grateful to its editor, Caitlin McCall, for her effervescent encouragement. Thanks also to Alice Wright, my editor at Bloomsbury, for her kindness in bringing this book into being.

The quotation in Chapter 13 from *Mistra: Byzantine capital of the Peloponnese* by Steven Runciman, © 1980 Thames and Hudson Ltd, London, is reproduced by kind permission of Thames & Hudson.

I always think of my family with gratitude as I confect these archaeological postcards, especially of my late mother and my father who from a patch of Arcadia in Wiltshire have read of my whereabouts in some foreign place often before they have heard me recount my tales of travel.

Giove, Umbria

June 2016

Introduction: An Archaeologist's Sense of the Past

Figure 1 Abbot Joshua (792–817) found in the excavations of the crypt of San Vincenzo Maggiore, August 1994 (courtesy John Mitchell).

'You must be very patient', almost everyone asserts admiringly on encountering an archaeologist. Patience in the pursuit of history instantly earns consideration. Patience to sift through the soil to discover treasure – from gold to unidentifiable knick-knacks – an educated beachcomber. Truth be told, patience does not come into it so much as the alchemy of experiences from being in the company of others as the five senses are tested and satisfied by the buried unexpected.

Archaeology is about hearing, seeing, smelling, tasting and touching past textures in our time. With these senses, in the company of friends, new places are created from old ones.

The experience of archaeology is transacted between the place today, with the sensuality of discovering history, and a nuanced narrative of its importance in the past (which is, of course, subject to contemporary interpretation). Best of all is the unravelling of these pasts in the company of fellow archaeologists. Mystical perhaps, there is a shared journey of discovery.

Some nostalgic illustrations: each of my excavations has involved the making of a bond with the past as well as the present. I began excavating as a teenager on a Roman villa in a small Wiltshire village. Now the villa and the village are entwined as I recall those digging days. Nearly 50 years later, the excavation resembles a pile of faded monochrome postcards: mud-like treacle settled around the sharp-edged sides of the trenches; hired workmen with flat caps teaching me how to flick a shovel and swing an Irish pickaxe; the diamond beauty of the phosphoric white microliths (flints), tempering the old Roman ground surface. The paramount memory fixed forever, cleaning down to the thin veneer of trapped grains immediately above a mosaic pavement for the first time. Removing the tell-tale veneer, easing away the finest sand like ants' eggs and the bleached tesserae laid two millennia before emerged from the edge of the trowel to be stroked, a carpet of stone, still rich in threaded colour and texture. The veneer and the excitement of its discovery first introduced to me by my mentor, Henry, remains more vivid than the patterning on the pavement itself. Here, I first encountered the company that belongs to an excavation: my strange and curious and energetic fellow diggers, and the local community – our benefactor, the gangly, serenely gentle Reverend Tom Selwyn Smith and Mary Lambert who provided warm scones and cream for each afternoon tea break.

There is so much more to the past than treasures. In a winter excavation of the Roman colonial levels deep beneath the shapeless anonymity of modern Gloucester we discovered the wooden drains of the Roman city. Charcoal-black, they were preserved intact in water-logged levels, a swamp of sorts. Each morning we smashed the ice, then pumped and bailed the molten water for an hour before gingerly conceding to kneeling in slime with trowels and cloths to peal back the faces of the 2,000 year-old wooden boards. The fetid smell and silky feel of these boards has stuck to me like the slime coating them for 40 years. They had the stretched febrile skin of a mummy, leather-hard of course, emitting a repugnant, dung-like odour. The intricate clockmaker's skill of the Roman carpenter was so unexpected. Tenon jointing as elegant as any Chippendale chair, and in this instance designed to serve civic interests. We would clean all day to reveal this prosaic marvel, defying the trickling rivelets of icy water, before allowing these treasures to return to their muddied haunts overnight.

Gloucester led to Knidos in south-west Turkey thanks to Henry. Knidos was a privilege for its sensual pleasures and those who peopled the excavation. The pervasive smell of thyme drifting in the precious breeze, the shape of islands floating above a hammered blue sea in the archipelago and the warm tender, strangely comforting, Hellenistic blocks of the precinct that defined my excavation, combined with the exultant cries of our workmen and their gifts of dripping honey torn from makeshift hives summon up my most enduring of archaeological memories.

Knidos – a rocky headland at the end of a long peninsula in southwestern Turkey. Charles Newton, sometime British consul to the Greek islands, had ruthlessly plundered this breathtaking ancient metropolis at the height of the Crimean War. With the help of Lord Palmerston, the British Prime Minister, he had acquired the frigate, *HMS Gorgon* that like a monster from a Greek myth transported many tonnes of Greek sculpture to London, today gracing the British Museum.

Knidos was paradise: kilometres of ruins occupied the hillslope overlooking the Dodecanese. Above all this had been a triumphant sanctuary for the sculptor, Praxiteles's seamark, a naked Aphrodite. The search for this ancient masterpiece, lost with the advent of Christianity, gave purpose to our excavations. Generations of peasants had added their own garnish to antiquity, fashioning small plots of tobacco, tilled by head-scarved women from the surrounding villages. Lingering sunsets occupying the horizon over the island of Kos provided the greatest of all spectacles in this unforgettable place.

As the August heat became more intense, the workmen resembling pirates, dressed in flimsy cotton akin to pyjamas, would sing. They began with local songs, then as the menace of weariness approached they would embark on makeshift verses about their leader, the *muktar* – a shadowless individual, his left eye supposedly reduced to a molten opaque colour by olive juice, and his mischievously open affair with an icy blond ceramics scholar from a German university. Some said she was peddling contraband and had inveigled the *muktar's* support on behalf of her Istanbul lover. Whatever the truth, these stories were grist to a hillside of boisterous singing that accelerated the digging. Undersized men pushing heavy wrought-iron barrows out onto precipitous mounds of dirt sang with the greatest gusto, hoping no doubt that their lusty refrains might tease others with thinner skins far below.

Kindos was my first experience of a dead place brought to life and more. It had been a metropolis in ancient times with great malls as well as two fine theatres, and a celebrated temple housing the brazen statue of Aphrodite. On a Monday morning a small army of men would arrive for roll-call at dawn, setting up a billowing cloud of dust along the corniche road leading into the city. The bedlam of men shouting, mules bellowing and attendant cockerels beckoned us from our cocoon. Until then we had been breakfasting since first light, as Newton did, basking in the splendour of this Aegean setting, but bearing baggage from our American, British, Italian and Turkish universities. Like an opera it ended with a dramatic climax and suddenly, after the approbation, this confected energy was gone, bequeathing a place with empty trenches to be partly sequestered by shrubs. When I returned decades later I found only a solitary guard. The spirit of the place remained in one sense, but in another its vitality had been eviscerated as surely as it had been lost when, with the fall of Rome's empire, the Arabs sacked Knidos and brutishly scrawled a graffito on the marble floor of its great church. Today yachtsmen slip into the anchorage here without knowing what we, who dug here, knew of its sensual treasures.

The sense of discovery also tells one something about oneself and one's spirit of enterprise.

My largest excavation was designed to uncover the crypt of a ninth-century Italian abbey, San Vincenzo Maggiore. Set on a hidden verdant plateau in Molise, half-surrounded by vertiginous mountains, a sardonic chronicle, the *Chronicon Vulturnense,* recalled the great history of this place as it was failing in the twelfth century. Centuries before the monastery had been a cosmopolitan city of god, a bespoke institution in the revival of post-classical Europe. Its fame, as in all great epics, induced the wrath of ages, in its case Saracens who sacked it on 10 October AD 881. Such vandalism, of course, provided us with an extraordinary opportunity. Building by building came to light, a Pompeii of sorts abandoned in a calamity, until I could calculate the bearings of the sacred heart of the place, its great church with a ring crypt in which the bones of St. Vincent, stolen from Umayadd Spain, were interred to create a cult and with it leveraged support for the monks. How did I know where the abbey-church was, professionals and amateurs asked me afterwards? In the long tradition of western rationalism, I made a scientific judgement based upon various fragments of archaeological and historical evidence. But that's being less than honest. As I took the decision to commit huge resources to this excavation of a featureless field I was conscious that long before Rosalina Iannotta, an eighty-year-old blind woman from these parts with olive-toned skin, led me through vineyards and groves to that exact spot to recount the horror of AD 881 and the existence of the great church where the fiercest battle occurred beneath our feet.

'Ecch ce sctèven 'gl 'riesct' de na grossa città, e sct posct seva la parte chiù importante,' she said in Molisano slang.

('Here the ruins of a great city once stood, and here was its most important part.')

It was almost as if she had seen the calamity with her own eyes eleven hundred years before. Could I really take her seriously? Should I have? A dozen years later her 'vision' was to give me a tacit sense of purpose. Five weeks into the dig in this empty field to find the abbey-church with a 50-strong army of excavators, naggingly little was apparent. Perhaps I had incorrectly interpreted the technical data because I wanted this church with its crypt to be there? Perhaps. The team lumbered on in the July heat, moving barrow-loads of rubble and mortared earth and, then, after ten weeks, the lower half of a magnificently painted crypt rose from the Medieval ground, as if prompted by some hidden force. How I wished Rosalinda could have been there. From the great trench amidst the sable colourlessness emerged frescoed splendours, the walls covered with a ravishing luminous palette of colours to match any illuminated bible or stained glass window. More than these deeply affecting colours, there was an unforgettable smell – a freshness of ochre, rich with pigment. More, concealed in two niches we cleaned away the rubble to expose the portraits of two abbots – chronicled fathers of the monastery's renascent age, each crowned by a square nimbus, dressed in simple brown robes with their hands statuesquely pressed towards the viewer in an orant posture. The long-buried abbots seemed startled to be so rudely thrust into the limelight. Such is the power and authority of these images captured in prayer that but for the old, blind peasant's encouragement to liberate this place I should have felt guilty about releasing their entombed spirits into the modern world. I mark this exultant discovery in the calendar of my mind each year – when nuns visited us to pay homage to their forebears, and when, later, an abbot with a scarlet skullcap and perfectly polished brogues along with assorted, saturnine politicians held a mass of sorts in memory of an age long-since forgotten by all except those who for generations had hoed this land. More than 20 years later I mull over in my mind was it the blind peasant's insistence that galvanized my decision to make this discovery?

Of course, discovery holds other prizes. The puzzle of ruins is far more challenging to the senses to resolve than any crossword. What do ruined walls or skewed rooms mean? Why did they build here? How did it end? More fascinating still is the search for the logic of transformation. How was a building modified and altered to become something entirely different? The rhythms of time and the inherent genesis of remaking places offer an inescapable fascination. The layers of soil, each with its own texture and smell, and the fragments of wall bear incontrovertible witness to a greater and very particular human history, if their logic can be decoded to construct a new narrative.

I left Knidos in a caique (not an imperial frigate) that glided in fits and starts across the combed blue expanse to Bodrum. I left with a longing, an itch, 'Mediterraneanism' I call it, that for years I failed to assuage. For 25 years afterwards I searched for the bundle of senses I had voraciously consumed there. This ended when I gazed across Lake Butrint on a warm, shimmering September morning towards the floating landscape around ancient Butrint in southern Albania.

Virgil's 'Troy in miniature' had been discovered by Luigi Maria Ugolini on behalf of Benito Mussolini. Between 1928 and 1936 Ugolini, with protean effort, created a great classical city from the bare hillsides before succumbing to a war wound at a ridiculously young age. Today, Butrint is much as he invented it, but blessed with a canopy of trees which, in this empty, treeless landscape, nurture a carpet of spring flowers and with them, squadrons of butterflies. Butrint, though, sublime as the archaeology and setting are, is majestic in my mind because the struggle to discover its past and protect the place has permitted me to play a small part in a larger struggle for Europe at the end of the twentieth century.

The complications of the story contain the purpose of placemaking and the pride I take from it as an archaeologist. In 1944, forgotten by the Great Powers in their wartime Yalta discussions, Albania was taken by communists led by Enver Hoxha. Hoxha transformed it into 'a paradise on this earth', an isolated state of repression. Shaping a pillar of this paradise, Hoxha's dictated that his archaeologists be prized academics, charged to discover Albania's unique origins in an (Iron Age) Illyrian tribal past even, improbably, at Graeco-Roman Butrint, ancient *Buthrotum*. With his demise and the subsequent fall of communism in 1992, this pocket-sized republic first defined in 1913 was beggared beyond belief. The scars of Hoxha's infinite repression were visible in the form of 600,000 bunkers disposed against a virtual enemy and invisibly deep in the minds of all its confused citizens. Anarchy reigned. One slim spectre of this anarchy survives in the UNESCO inscription of Butrint as a world heritage site, dating from 1992. Unaware of any ethnic issues, UNESCO inscribed Butrint as essentially a Greek place, as though the Greek minority splinter republic of 1914–1915 – Epirus Vetus – had lived on, undeterred by the brutal passage of Hoxha's repressive totalitarianism.

Faced with a narrative for Butrint that Ugolini designed and an Illyrian one invented by Hoxha's nationalist cronies, as well as one for overt political mischief innocently adopted by UNESCO, none of which made sense to any visitor, I set about seeking a Mediterranean narrative for this quintessential Mediterranean place. At first there was no meeting of minds with our collaborators. Their isolationist ideology was unshakeable, while their workmen fished with dynamite and stole our equipment, such was the abject poverty in spirit and fact. For them, digging was purely mercenary labour. With patient fortitude, navigating the national and local currents, over a decade we dissolved their ideology and discovered a new narrative. Our archival research, our surveys of the hinterland around Butrint, our study of the ancient environments, and the privilege of excavating large and small trenches inside and outside the walled town provided us with the ammunition to describe the rise and fall and rise and fall of this place up until its zenith today as a sensual shrine to modern tourism. The compressed jumble of walls, interlaced with thick layers to gain elevation above rising spring waters was, at first, hard to read. Certain periods of the urban story defined by major monuments and well-known construction techniques were easily interpreted. But most periods bequeathed spare and vestigial traces, less easily read and explained. Only as a common picture emerged in numerous trenches was the vicissitudinous storyline of the place evident and the puzzle solved. Much condensed, this narrative is to be found on the colourful site panels we erected, as well as in the selectivity and arrangement of the museum display we constructed in 2005. Responsive to the tourist's gaze we shaped a story of a small Mediterranean hilltop that won fame, thanks to Octavian's (later, the Emperor Augustus) association with grandees here, and with Virgil's stanzas intricately bound to the foundation myth of Rome itself. In Late Antiquity, in the Middle Ages and even in Ottoman times, Virgil's shadow had a status that often far exceeded the importance of Butrint. Thanks to Virgil's lines about 'lofty' Butrint, Ugolini steadfastly brought its constellation of Roman and Byzantine monuments back to life, and the happenstance of the woodland canopy graced these ruins with a nimbus that to most qualifies as sacred. This narrative of town life through time and form, confronting lagoonal marshes over many centuries, rings closer to the worldview of today's charmed visitors.

Now Butrint is on the traveller's map. For today's foreign visitors its recent struggle with tyranny is measured hospitably by this blissful oasis in a Homeric landscape. Albanian tourists, 25 years after Communism fell, are intrigued by other senses. There is the sight of ruins in a bucolic woodland untroubled by the degradation of their towns; the smell of wild flowers pollinated by hosts of butterflies; the silence of the wood magnified by the interrupting cry of a successful fisherman beyond it; the tender taste of fresh fish – *cozze*, languishing shoals to be plucked wriggling from the channel here; the touch of the hewn seats in the Hellenistic theatre, comfortingly warm and polished by backsides for millennia. This precious sense of place protects the archaeology, and now celebrated, it is much more profound because it lives on. Albanians come here to get married. Here, where our new archaeological narrative challenges Virgil's myth ascribing Butrint's origin to Trojan exiles, our intervention in one way or another provided a new Butrint with an aura permitting brides and grooms to take ownership of this place.

An archaeologist's past is woven of such textures from the discovery of a mosaic pavement or an ancient drain to invoking the authority of a new Mediterranean narrative. My own genesis in neatly cut trenches at Box, Gloucester, Knidos, San Vincenzo and Butrint (as well as other places) has shaped my assignations with archaeology. The colours of soil, in sun and rain; the discoveries of benchmarks in history; and, above all, the making of places in the company of friends and colleagues, knowing that they will live on but never quite as fully without the vitality of these people. Field reports and monographs never tell this tale, but it is the pursuit of these senses that compels me to dig and, when travelling, to search for bearings in the past. Finding such senses, to paraphrase the poet Seamus Heaney, an ardent lover of antiquity and archaeology, motivates my 'squat pen'.

In the Company of Placemaking People

2

In Charles Newton's Shadow: Searching for Demeter at Knidos

Figure 2 Knidos: View of the headland from the overgrown terraces, 2011.

'There is something very attractive in this place – the delicious freshness of the air, the beauty of the scenery, the stir and activity of our little colony in the midst of such loneliness and ruin ... The sea-view here is much more lively than at Budrum, as we have a glimpse of all that passes up and down on the great highway between the Dardanelles and Rhodes. The French and Austrian steamers going to and fro with letters, almost within hail of us, are a cheerful sight, one of the pleasantest that can gladden the heart of an exile.'

(C.T. Newton, *Travels and Discoveries in the Levant,* London, 1865, 162)

I have returned to Knidos after 40 years. Across the decades you forget the outlines of the trenches and the stratigraphic relationships these contained. Instead, Knidos remains etched in my memory as a panorama encompassing the suggestive silhouettes of many of the Dodecanese islands, as well as the brilliant crystalline blue expanse of the Aegean. The ancient city lies at the tip of a long mountainous finger of land pointing out into this sea; it is as unexpected as it is magical. Today, as 40 years ago, because the twisting road along the corniche is so narrow and perilous, most visitors arrive by yacht, anchoring in the Hellenistic commercial harbour just past the ancient moles. Modern Knidos amounts to very little. Ruşan's restaurant remains at the terminus of the makeshift jetty; Mehmet's café remains too, though it is no longer a shack. There is a *jandarma* for the military and a modest store for the excavation finds. This gaggle of buildings is dwarfed by the scale of the sprawling Hellenistic and Byzantine city. The ancient city rises up like a theatre on countless terraces, occupying the last three kilometres of the peninsula as well as the adjoining islet of Cape Crio where a Victorian lighthouse marks the farthest tip of this lost metropolis.

Forty years ago I was unbelievably lucky to get the opportunity as a first-year undergraduate to dig at Knidos. The overture to the excavation set the scene for this long summer: the train from London to Rome, my first visit to the British School at Rome, the long drive by landrover past Monte Cassino to Brindisi, an overnight Adriatic Sea ferry to Igoumenitsa, the tortuous mountain road past Metsovo to Salonika, the plains of Thrace, crossing the Dardanelles at night to sleep at Troy, procuring the excavation equipment in the Izmir bazaar, and then the momentous drive in a Willy's jeep to Knidos tracing the coastline along mule tracks, culminating after a week of travelling with the sun setting in a blaze of fire over Cape Crio.

As with all digs, there was a galaxy of unlikely personalities, assembled by the celebrated American director of the project – characters who, in retrospect, educated me in this improbable finishing school on life as well as classical archaeology. Today, I remember them with gratitude: I was the youngest of a field team numbering around 25, and apart from the pot-washing boys, much younger than the legion of upwards of 100 men hired from the neighbouring villages. We slept in tents on the narrow beach in the lea of Cape Crio and ate and worked in a modest dig-house close by. There was one electrical light, a makeshift shower from a single pipe of water, and a 'loo with a view' which attracted a menacing multitude of flies. This was full immersion in an archaeological odyssey.

Charles Newton had excavated at Knidos on behalf of the British Government in 1857–1858. Following legislation passed by Prime Minister Palmerston at the height of the Crimean war, Newton, a junior keeper in the British Museum, was granted a frigate and a company of sappers in order to obtain a consignment of sculptures from the ancient city. First Newton made a small fortress to secure his team from local brigands; he then mapped and excavated Knidos with Victorian resolution. Tonnes of rock were displaced and tonnes of marble sculpture were loaded onto *HMS Gorgon* including the 8-tonne hollow-eyed lion (from atop a grandiose Hellenistic tomb) which today mounts guard in the Great Court of the British Museum. Other Knidian treasures also grace the British Museum, notably a fine statue of the goddess, Demeter.

I knew nothing of this Demeter when I arrived in July 1971 to be dispatched, with ten workmen and their mules, to excavate the temenos where Charles Newton had found the goddess that he shipped home. Charles Newton was spell-bound by this statue:

'The features and form are those of an elderly woman wasted with sorrow, and do not exhibit that matronly comeliness and maturity of form which usually characterize Demeter in ancient art.'

She also captivated the novelist, E.M. Forster who journeyed to Knidos one winter's day. On reaching the temenos Forster mused thoughtfully on the goddess:

'She was there [in the British Museum] at that moment, warm and comfortable in that little recess of hers between the Ephesian Room and the Archaic Room, with the electric light fizzling above her, and casting blue shadows over her chin. She is dusted twice a week, and there is a railing in front, with "No Admittance", so that she cannot be touched. And if human industry can find that lost arm of hers, and that broken nose, and human ingenuity can put them on, she shall be made as good as new.'

E.M. Forster, Cnidus, *Abinger Harvest*, London,
Edward Arnold, 1936, 171–72.

My task in 1971, I now suspect (though no-one said so at the time), was to find those limbs.

Today I followed the winding path across the many deserted terraces, once planted with tobacco, captivated by the terrain now reduced to a mixture of small stones and ancient potsherds. Far beyond the main centre of the metropolis, settled below a sheer rock face, is the terrace, now overgrown with thorns, where Newton's team discovered the Demeter and much more besides. From here there is a mighty spectacle. Out over the sea to the west lies the long spindly island of Kos: Lawrence Durrell called it the spoiled child of the Dodecanese. It remains ever a green enchanted place staring at Halicarnassos, modern Bodrum, on the Turkish mainland, and sharing with it a mighty crusader castle. Beyond the lighthouse on Cape Crio, lies Nicyros, its extinct volcano sharpest in the hazy morning light. The seascape then dims into the horizon staining the sky before the next island, Tilos, today only a distant land mass.

Knidos has a strong affinity with these islands. It, too, seems like an island, bobbing gently in the eastern Aegean, sharing in the serene glow that indefinably brightens this region. The roots of this affinity, however, are deep. Knidos with the three great cities of Rhodes – Lindos, Ialysos and Kamiros – as well as with Kos and Halicarnassos was a member of the Dorian Hexapolis. Herodotus, a native of Halicarnassos in the fifth century, tells us about this association, and their games, paying tribute to Knidos as the largest of the cities. It was here, he tells us, that the great temple to Apollo was the common sanctuary of the Hexapolis.

Ancient Knidos, as Newton and successive excavators have shown, was a metropolis housing tens of thousands of people. In the fifth century BC Hippodamos of Miletus, the greatest architect of his age, designed the new city at Knidos, aiming to emulate those of Priene and Miletus, further up the coast, just as he had designed the new Piraeus. The new Knidos covered an area about three kilometres long and roughly a kilometre wide. It is impossible to imagine: straight, paved, parallel streets traversing the hillsides, separating monumental ashlar buildings erected like Manhattan skyscrapers. Now few places better summon up the natural beauty of the Aegean and, stripped of these ancient malls, the fragile sustainability of human enterprise.

Today I determined to seek out my trenches, laid out with the help of my jester, Mumtaz Sariyaz, the effervescent supervisor of the workmen. A wiry man, all bones, with deep-set eyes and a shock of black hair, he introduced me to his benign world of peasant values. We had cleared the temenos of the thorns to reveal its elevated front wall made of Hellenistic blocks cut from conglomerate. A mountain of broken stone ran back to the sharp steep rear wall of the terrace, scree brought down by an earthquake after Newton's time. The rock face itself, though, was unchanged after 150 years, punctured by two sharply cut niches intended for statues.

Over the course of two months we excavated long trenches to reveal the deep terrace fills on which a podium wall of the temple to Demeter had been constructed. The cyclopean construction was immense, unmoveable, and exactly as I had left it. Today, these deep holes are easily traced; the stratigraphy, too, is patently obvious. Newton, I discovered, had erased almost everything with characteristic if not fanatical diligence. My team and I were bequeathed only tell-tale black-glazed potsherds that enabled us to date the making of the temenos and add a footnote to the story of the Demeter that seduced Forster. Did it really matter that we found no marble limbs of Demeter, or a fragment of her nose? Not to Mumtaz and his men, who loved the airiness of the elevated temenos and the relaxed direction I administered. Not to me, endlessly enchanted by this extraordinary setting for a dig.

From the temenos, in the 'gods' of this Knidian theatre all the ancient city lay before me. I could descend before the sun splashed into the sea to visit the Hellenistic stepped-street excavations, or I could follow the goatherd paths along the high contours past the monumental theatre to the round temple where, with dynamite, the sanctuary that housed Praxiteles' famed statue of a naked Aphrodite was discovered. Today, it is this little ashlar-made monument that draws the yachting crowd, as it did 40 years ago. The salty aroma from plants sprayed by the sea along with the suggestion that this ancient Aphrodite thrilled many an ancient visitor has an enduring attraction. But truth to tell, the abiding fascination of Knidos is the spirit of a metropolis reborn as a blissful seascape wherein a multitude of monuments and stories, despite Charles Newton's best efforts, remain secreted.

3

Wim van Es and the Discovery of the Dutch 'Troy', Dorestad

Figure 3 Dorestad: Combined city gate and windmill leading into the modern town of Wijk bij Duurestede.

Troy is not a place one normally associates with Holland. Yet the Dutch claim to have their own Troy: Dorestad. It lies at the point where the Rhine parts company with the river Lek, about 100 kilometres south-east of Amsterdam. The picturesque town of modern Wijk bij Duurestede does not attract many visitors, yet it is the site of one of Europe's greatest towns, a place closely associated with the very making of Europe.

Today, Wijk bij Duurestede is a dormitory town for nearby Utrecht. First appearances are not misleading: there is a fine Romanesque castle, majestically built in brick, and a walled late Medieval centre dominated by an early baroque church. Like many Dutch towns everything about it is well appointed. Flower baskets grace many of the cobbled streets and the older houses have been discretely restored. But this unassuming place has a history worthy of Troy.

Its modern history began in the mid-nineteenth century when some of its citizens were starving. As a last resort some turned to digging up the bone pits in their gardens that they knew dated back to ancient times. The remains of animals butchered more than 1,000 years earlier were boiled to make the thinnest broths. With the bones came a plethora of artefacts including coins, breathing fresh life into the sketchy history of a huge riverside market that was formerly home to Frisian merchants. These discoveries had added significance as historians of the Low Countries late in the nineteenth century identified these Argonauts of the North Sea as the first Medieval merchant-venturers.

From the seventh to the ninth centuries, as Europe was being reconfigured to take its familiar Medieval and modern configurations, the Frisian diaspora managed a triangular trading zone between the German rivers, Anglo-Saxon England and the western Baltic. Operating out of Dorestad, a precursor of modern Rotterdam, these merchants fuelled an appetite for Anglo-Saxon woollens and Scandinavian furs in Charlemagne's empire, and fed it with German goods manufactured in Rhineland factory villages. So started a relationship with the Rhineland that still accounts for much of the wealth in the Netherlands today.

J.H. Holwerda made the first excavations at Dorestad in 1922, establishing that the Frisian artefacts belonged to large riverside properties. A reconstruction made for the excavator projects the excavated remains as though this were a baroque castle with fortifications and a fixity that belied the excavated evidence. These discoveries were soon trumpeted by grateful historians as proof of the rise of Charlemagne's Europe and its bold entrepreneurs. It is difficult today to grasp the significance of this: perhaps the simplest illustration is that as the Netherlands fell to the Nazi invaders in May 1940, SS officer and archaeologist, Herbert Jankuhn breathlessly attempted to revive the excavations. Such was Dorestad's perceived importance to the Dutch psyche that its parliament, notwithstanding the blitzkrieg and the mayhem caused by the invasion, caucused to prevent Jankuhn's initiative … and succeeded in doing so. Protected by river silts, Dorestad survived for another era.

Dorestad was re-born in the modern age thanks to the young director of the Dutch State Archaeological Service, Wim van Es. Faced with a plan for a gigantic housing development scheme at Wijk bij Duurstede, growing the village of 3,500 to 25,000 inhabitants, this brilliant archaeologist mustered his forces to run one of the largest excavations of the modern age. Between 1967 and 1978, working with machinery and a small year-round team, van Es decided not to salvage a small portion of the ground given over to the new dwellings, but instead to uncover a staggering 55 hectares. As a result, for the first time, the topography of an early Medieval emporium was unearthed. A Babylonian wealth of finds was now complemented by an understanding of the town plan of this Frisian capital. The Dutch Troy was given real definition.

These stupendous excavations showed that the river had moved, leaving the old town to the archaeologists. The Dorestad that emerged comprised a line of wooden jetties supported on timber piles, beyond which lay a thin ribbon of riverside buildings. Set back from this meandering port was a nucleus of major farm buildings, each occupying its own fenced enclosure. Apart from the massive bow-shaped timber and thatched dwellings, typical of farms in the Rhine delta region, each household possessed one or more wells made of stave-made timber barrels produced using timber from the southern Rhineland.

Van Es put Dorestad on the map. I visited him many times in the 1970s, thrilled by his capacity for bringing the Dark Ages and the world of Charlemagne and King Offa to light. His melting smile was irresistible as was his sharp wit. My involvement went deeper: in 1977 he examined my doctoral thesis and invited me to publish a major essay in the Dutch state journal. In 1979, we made a BBC Radio 4 programme at Dorestad in the little site museum. His capacity as a placemaker, bringing to life the lost metropolis known in the Middle Ages as *Vicus Famosus*, was inspiring. Thanks to his single-minded efforts, Dorestad has become the cornerstone of early Medieval archaeology north of the Alps.

Dorestad lives on past van Es's retirement. A new project to digitally assemble all the material excavated in the past has been accompanied by a new excavation. Called the Odyssee project, the circumstances in Wijk bij Duurstede could not be more different from the phenomenal salvage drive by van Es. On a glorious early autumnal day we met with his team and local officials in the town hall where everyone, naturally, speaks fluent English. Then, led by Wilfried Hessing, a veteran of van Es's project, and the mastermind of Odyssee, we walked across the ground once covered by the old fruit and vegetable market – the Veilingterrein – an area of nearly four hectares recently excavated by Juke Dijkstra and Gavin Williams. As we ambled on, I quizzed my companions about the controversial history of van Es's dig: the developers were mightily miffed by the archaeologists who delayed the housing construction. On we continued through leafy lanes beside well-tended back yards to the riverside, where on the far side a Roman fort secured the delta and served as the nucleus for a seventh–ninth-century administrator who controlled the customs dues for all who traded along the jetties. These were people like Ibbo who in the ninth century sailed with four boats from Trier to England, passing through Dorestad. On we strolled to the towering Romanesque donjon, before turning back into the walled town to attend a round table briefing session in a hall. Here I was treated to two hours on the recent discoveries: once more I was thrilled by the sheer scale of the archaeology and its international and historical reach.

The Veilingterrein area was excavated during 2007–2008. With time to work carefully, a strategy radically different to van Es's was employed. Where he had been compelled to machine away much to obtain the basic elements of the town, Dijkstra and Williams with their team were encouraged to go more slowly. Not surprisingly, a new, more nuanced picture of Frisian townlife has emerged. Two results stand out. First, this inner sector of the metropolis was occupied by three farms in their grand compounds from the foundation of Dorestad in the late seventh century until the later eighth century. This insula of Dorestad was then re-fashioned as seven dwellings, most of which were associated with crafts of one kind or another. Dorestad plainly prospered as Charlemagne's renaissance within his empire created a huge demand for imported materials. Second, the Babylonian quantities of finds produced by van Es's excavations were dwarfed by these more controlled excavations. Perhaps the most astonishing discovery is the assemblage of 40 Carolingian coins, minted by Charlemagne and his son – many at Dorestad with their signature boat motif. This first euro (agreed at the Council of Frankfurt in AD 793) was plainly as popular as its modern iteration, being imitated directly in Denmark by Viking communities and as far south as Benevento in southern Italy (though the English opted out of an exact imitation ...). The many lost coins in this backstreet of craftsmen at Dorestad show that the Frisian traders were eager proponents of a unified monetary economy! Of course, this euro mark 1 failed as the Vikings descended upon north-west Europe, though many might say that political squabbling really caused its downfall. Whatever, these new excavations complement van Es's mammoth digs; together, they tell an arresting European story pertinent to our troubled times.

According to the historical stories, Dorestad, like Troy, fell victim to outsiders. In this Dutch case these were Viking marauders rather than Homeric warriors in search of Helen. The excavations, well-dated by dendrochronology – the dating of the tree rings – together with myriad coins, show that this mighty mercantile engine faltered and suddenly declined before the Vikings arrived. Had demand in post-Charlemagne Germany suddenly dried up? Was the market for Carolingian goods in Anglo-Saxon England saturated? The debate continues, but today with incontrovertible evidence.

Dorestad will never be the tourist trap that is Troy. But any visitor to its little museum and its subtly signposted past will get a powerful sense of the long shadow reaching from Carolingian times to our age. As we followed the cobbled streets on this blissful autumnal day, musing on contemporary Europe's woes, I was reminded that German-made Mercedes-Benz currently contributes to Rotterdam's prosperity – the modern Dorestad – though these cars are shipped to China. I wondered aloud whether in these gigantic collections of finds from the old and modern digs if there is a Chinese object, yet to be identified, that directly connects this Dutch Troy to the country's present affluence.

4

Johnny Mitchell and San Vincenzo al Volturno's First Saint

Figure 4 A fresco depicting a young saint that changed the course of the excavations at San Vincenzo al Volturno (courtesy John Mitchell).

Thirty years ago my career took a memorable new turn. I had been trained in settlement archaeology and the theory and practice that this entailed. Much of this was controversial because I subscribed to the so-called 'New Archaeology' championed by a generation of American archaeologists and emulated with some skill by the rising stars of British prehistory. These near-evangelical approaches were rooted in a search for a science of archaeology. However, how people in the past thought or expressed themselves in visual or written forms was considered rather old fashioned. There was perhaps a reason for this: few of us ever had the chance as archaeologists to discover paintings or texts. Our bread and butter were the barest of ruins and essentially prosaic finds. Then, on 1 September 1981, during the second year of my excavations at San Vincenzo al Volturno – 120 miles south of Rome – I encountered a truly unexpected challenge to all I believed.

The challenge came in the ebullient form of John Mitchell, an art historian and then lecturer at the University of East Anglia, Norwich. I had invited him (without meeting him!) to help interpret a painted altar found during the first season of excavations (in 1980). I forewarned the team of diehard diggers to be polite, presumptuously assuming art historians to be precious, unlike the down-and-dirty archaeologists. Boy, I was wrong: he arrived with his old rucksack, brimming with unalloyed eagerness to be back at San Vincenzo where 10 years before he had slept in an olive grove after visiting the celebrated and isolated painted crypt of Epyphanius. Before the night was out, he was teaching the digging pirates new party games involving any amount of our 'rot-gut' red wine, leaving everyone bemused by my earlier cautiousness. His arrival was the catalyst for a bigger revelation. On that very day the excavations had ventured into a new sector. Plunging deeper and bewilderingly deeper we came upon a tip of painted plaster fragments heaped back towards a brightly painted wall. John, with the eye of a professional, could scarcely believe we did not grasp what we had. Finding a huge aluminium baking tray and some builder's sand, he placed in it the painted fragments and rearranged them again and again – the first of countless hours spent on room-sized jigsaw puzzles. Like magic, our alchemist confected a saint's head. Confidently painted in ochrous bright colours, this bold-eyed individual revealed to us, so-to-speak, a very big story: we had found the vaunted ninth-century monastery of San Vincenzo al Volturno, described in picturesque detail in the twelfth-century *Chronicon Vulturnense.*

Our saint, we eventually learned, had graced the wall of a redecorated ground-floor atrium – the so-called Vestibule – that served as an intermediary room between a Beneventan palace occupying the north end of the Dark Age monastery and a sprawling, decorated, grandiose claustrum. On 1 September 1981, we discovered the tip of an iceberg that now reaches its final chapter

30 years later with a major monograph by John and I (with our endearingly patient research assistant, Sarah Leppard). From that day 30 years ago I have had to grasp the role of paintings and text, as well as the place of the minor arts of craftsmen, in the making of a Middle Ages which was, as the excavations at San Vincenzo al Volturno spectacularly showed, rich in detail and ever-changing ideas and imagination. The one-dimensional New Archaeology, with its suspicion of cognition and the role of the individual in the past, never again held the same appeal for me. All this I owe to John's effervescent tuition, which is why I have returned on this early spring day to find a detail pertinent to an essay – a footnote so-to-speak – that John and I are completing.

I always forget to mention that San Vincenzo al Volturno sits in the most majestic of settings. It's hard not to imagine the centuries of monks from Paldo, Tato and Taso onwards, who came here in 703, awakening with the dawn and gasping at the sight of the towering Mainarde mountains rising like a wall a mile or two away. Today, on this visit, deep snow is draped across the highest parts of this massif, merging dreamily into the crystalline sky. In the foreground stands Castel San Vincenzo, the quintessential hilltop town, almost floating in this benign early spring light. But my destination is the monastery that granted the village its foundation charter in AD 962. My discoveries in early September 1981 were made beside the river Volturno, now little more than a sparkling brook, half a mile from the present, so-called 'New Abbey', reconstructed after the Second World War. The discovery of the saint's head was the first affirmation that the celebrated monastery was not secreted below the present abbey reconstructed to affect its twelfth-century Romanesque iteration, but instead beside the river after which it took its name. Here, beyond a humped-back Roman bridge known as the Ponte della Zingara (the gypsy bridge), which spans the Volturno, was a well-preserved painted crypt of Epyphanius – its cycle of frescoes dating to the 830s. The crypt is too precious to be kept open these days – a special letter is required from the Abbot of Monte Cassino to visit it. To its immediate south, though, trench by trench, area by area, for 18 years, we discovered the exceptionally preserved remains of the ninth-century cloister and its great church, San Vincenzo Maggiore.

Today, two large excavations remain uncovered below steel shelters within which elevated walkways lead the visitor to where legions of students slaved in the summer sun. The walkways zig-zag along the highest parts, past the princely palace of about AD 800 – the best preserved of its era in Europe, to the tile-paved cloisters of the Carolingian age, the only ones yet exposed by archaeologists, to the great church of San Vincenzo Maggiore, with its annular crypt like those still visited in Rome at churches like Santa Prassede and S.S. Quattro Coronati, to the monastic workshops where the ninth-century monks, under a chamberlain's eye, made precious souvenirs for feudal-age donors to the monastery.

As a visiting Cassinese monk commented 30 years ago, everything about this archaeology is worthy of a Dark Age Pompeii. Here, though, the cataclysm was wrought not by a volcano but by an eruption of envy as Athanasius, Bishop of Naples, manipulated a Saracen warband to sack San Vincenzo on 10 October 881. Paradoxically, as a result of that heinous alliance, much of the monastery, thereafter abandoned, survived to be unearthed by our excavations.

Tidied up and blessed with neat and informative panels, this early Medieval monastic city is now open to the public (every morning except Mondays). Entry is free, but the authorities ask visitors to sign a book. Flicking through its pages, the signatories are all local, here at weekends for picnics, venturing beyond the New Abbey, my next port of call.

The New Abbey was founded half a mile away in the twelfth century. Defended by deep ditches on two sides, the new monastery was intentionally a break with that sacked by the Saracens. However, it never flourished and by the Second World War when it was bombed, the grand church had been sorely reduced in scale. Angelo Pantoni, a monk and antiquarian at Monte Cassino, oversaw the post-war reconstruction, returning it to its ambitious twelfth-century form. For a time, Pantoni had me persuaded that the early Medieval monastery founded in 703 and sacked in 881 was here too. With time, as the ninth-century ruins emerged in my dig, Pantoni, the most gracious of historians, acknowledged that there were, in fact, earlier and later monasteries. But Pantoni's pastiche failed too until Monte Cassino granted it to a small community of nuns from the Abbey of Regina Laudis in Connecticut in 1990. Led by Mother Miriam with Mothers Agnes and Philip, they have been spiritual catalysts for change at San Vincenzo, giving this place spiritual leadership.

On this spring visit Mother Philip opened the monastery gate and hugged me: she excavated for years on the excavations and has a chapter on the flints in our forthcoming monograph. Next we find Mother Miriam, the prioress, busying about her work in her denim habit: the sparkle in her eyes unquenched by the years of struggle to sustain the community. Next, they find Mother Agnes, an indefatigable figure who within moments is deep in conversation about the book bindings we found abandoned during the Saracen attack. The trio are infused with equal amounts of charm and strength that is as much a blissful balm as the day and countryside itself. Over coffee we recall our excavations together, the endlessly complicated personalities and endemic obstacles of this otherwise gentle corner of southern Italy. My mind drifts, inevitably, across two decades to recall their enthralled faces as they sang a hymn over the first traces of the hitherto lost crypt of San Vincenzo Maggiore, after John Mitchell and I excitedly explained the meaning of the frescoes emerging in the first trial trenches. There and then the Dark Age Pompeii was spiritually alive once more.

As I acknowledged to the three beaming nuns, my life changed on 1 September 1981. Few discoveries of early Medieval archaeology have been as evocative and magical, resonant with individuals – artists and bookbinders – as well as chronicled abbots, continuing today with the nuns. Then, too, few discoveries have been infused with more enthusiasm, wit and spirit, than those involving these three nuns and my irrepressible colleague, John Mitchell.

5

Riccardo and Quinto – Placemaking at 'Lost' Tuscan Villages

Figure 5 Riccardo Francovich at 60, 10 June 2006.

West of Siena, after the straggling village of Rosia, the main road for Massa Marittima and the Tyrrhenian coast passes through a twisting gorge. This tract of road connects the centre of Tuscany to its western reaches. On exiting the gorge, proud on a bluff to the right lies Montarrenti. It is a quintessential hilltop village, though in this case, only one inhabitant remains – Quinto with his lean hunting dogs, fluffy rabbits and countless chickens. Quinto was, in fact, the only resident when in September 1981 we first slogged up the dusty track through the concentric circles of ruined fortifications to the two elegant towers separated by the stump of a third. In his thick Tuscan brogue he willingly linked arms with my companionable colleague, Riccardo Francovich and led us up, first, to the greater of the two towers – a palace on the west side, worthy of any Sienese grandee; then into and up the lesser tower, a slender one-period Romanesque building of exquisite proportions. Following this, we slid down the scree of age-old refuse below the towers – sending boulders, rusty tins and fragments of nineteenth-century chamber pots tumbling downwards. Below, occupying the girth of the hill, was a ring of well-made thirteenth-century peasant houses – each the size of a manor house in England at the time. The canopy of tall trees lent a forbidding spirit to this forgotten place. But the effervescent Riccardo was thrilled. With diminutive, bright-eyed Quinto by his side, he was in his element.

Six great seasons of excavations transformed Montarrenti. First, a great fence was erected to contain 12 deer – a cost-effective method of maintaining the vegetation. Then, there were the digs: an area of the hilltop was stripped down to the bare rock, as were three dwellings below. Colossal rock-piles were shifted to reveal the long history of a village that at first we assumed had been occupied in the later tenth century – the age of *incastellamento* (village building). Riccardo, however, increasingly questioned his own assumptions and during the fourth season in September 1985, a dwelling (Area 2000) on the lower girth was excavated to its earliest period. Structurally it was quite unlike the later, familiar, house made with ashlar and containing a ground-floor stable. (The kind of dwelling to be seen all over Tuscany today.) What we had found instead was a building cut into the natural rock with a few associated post-holes to take the uprights that supported a simple thatched roof. Indeed, excluding any thought of the later houses on this spot, the earliest was a sunken hut like those from Anglo-Saxon England or indeed much of the North Sea littoral.

With the irrepressible belief in the adventure that marked Riccardo as an extraordinary archaeologist, he charged me to obtain carbon 14 dates for other comparably early levels at Montarrenti. Faint-heartedly I did as instructed, and sure enough, the results confirmed Riccardo's hunch – we were uncovering the beginnings of a village that ante-dated the tenth century. Indeed, as we were to later show, its origins lay in the sixth or seventh century.

Never one to hold back, Riccardo organized a great conference in 1988 to challenge the very historians who had established the ideas that actually led us to Montarrenti! The incomparable gastronomic hospitality of Siena drew our unsuspecting colleagues to an encounter where Riccardo, with a characteristic mix of humour and scientific gravitas, challenged the accepted history of village formation in Italy. In practice, this involved an unforgettable verbal jousting match with the-then senior professor of Medieval history in the Sorbonne, Paris – Pierre Toubert. A rotund and austerely thoughtful man, who expressed himself in razor-like sentences, Toubert found the bombast from my Tuscan colleague mildly amusing but unacceptable. His (French) archaeologists, he reminded the star-struck ensemble, had also found post-holes, but these belonged to primitive dwellings that confirmed his biblical *magnum opus* on the subject. His archaeologists, we noted, nodded dutifully, as their master poured cold water on the challenging discoveries of Montarrenti. The unmoveable simply could not be moved. Riccardo, needless to say, was not to be intimidated by this great authority and his francophone grandiloquence, and so began a new era! We will show you, he genially ventured. After that meeting, Riccardo's pupils excavated more than a dozen hilltops like Montarrenti over the following 20 years and, by the mid-1990s, Toubert gracefully conceded that his hypothesis needed drastic revision.

This chapter in Italian history was uppermost in my mind as I paid my annual visit to Marco Valenti's extraordinary excavations at Miranduolo (in the locality of Chiusdino) in chestnut woods, ten miles west of Montarrenti. Close to the brick-built Cistercian abbey of San Galgano, often I had come to this unsuspecting archaeological haven with Riccardo. This time I was alone as my great friend had tragically died in an accident in March. One of his students drove us up the one-in-three incline to the dig deep in the thick woods. Beyond, in a clearing bathed in radiant sunlight, lay seven years of exposed remains, remarkable for taking the Montarrenti story and embellishing it spectacularly.

Marco tells a great story about this anonymous woodland. Miranduolo was little more than a rocky knoll when the first sunken huts were built on it. It is hard to imagine, yet this gaggle of buildings, as at Montarrenti, became the core of a community which grew and prospered in different guises over the following 600–700 years. Strip away the hill and the gently swaying chestnuts, and the village resembled West Stow (the now reconstructed village in Suffolk excavated in the 1960s) in size and shape. Riccardo's bombastic conviction about Montarrenti growing up like the Anglo-Saxon villages he had read so much about is now plain to see on the rocky terrain at Miranduolo. Like Montarrenti, the little community was transformed in the later ninth century when a manor house supplanted one sunken building and, more to the point, established its importance by excavating an extraordinary ditch to separate itself from the other dwellings. Alongside the manor, bell-shaped silos were excavated in the rock to store grain, large quantities of which, mostly burnt for storage purposes, have been found.

The manor now became the epicentre of the place. In the tenth century it was enclosed by a major, if simply made, wall. It was then acquired in the age of *incastellamento*, so the written sources affirm, by the powerful Gherardeschi family who controlled much of western Tuscany. Their impact is plain to see: a massive palatial tower replaced the manor house, dwarfing the cluster of dwellings beyond the ditch. Such conspicuous architectural authority soon attracted dissenters in the form of the neighbouring Bishop of Volterra who, between 1125 and 1133 laid siege to the palace and, as numerous arrowheads attest, led to its partial destruction. The Gherardeschi refurbished parts of their tower, but clearly they had lost faith in Miranduolo and eventually sold the property in 1257–1258 to local counts, the Cantoni of Montieri. Evidently the new family were not impressed and, as new farmhouses were constructed on the fertile plains around the region, and Miranduolo, on these unpropitious slopes, was abandoned.

Marco's vivid story – much of which can be read online as the diggers report through a blog during the season – is made all the more compelling by the netherworld of this secreted, sylvan spot. Unlike Montarrenti, there is no Quinto through whom one might forge a link to the past. However, here lies the chance to unearth much of the long sequence found at Montarrenti down the road. More importantly, the genesis of this settlement – from a cluster of huts, to a manor, then a palace – is evocatively clear and beyond doubt. This village long pre-dated the first tenth-century charters that Pierre Toubert described as the process of *incastellamento*. Indeed, as Marco says with the enthusiasm and passion of his teacher, our much-missed friend Riccardo, this place grew out of the last Roman villages and was peopled by peasants. Here, then, as at Montarrenti, began the making of Medieval Tuscany.

As we left the hilltop, I recalled to Marco – a youthful veteran of Montarrenti – how I had not really believed Riccardo as he danced with delight on the sides of the first hut (in Area 2000) we found in 1985 and with cheerful glee claimed that this would change history. The excavators, I recalled, had looked at him and beamed, not sure if he was brilliant or mad, utterly infected by his glorious passion. How he had been emphatically proved right! Marco smiled knowingly at my recollections. At Montarrenti, and now at Miranduolo, we agreed, what really fired Riccardo's imagination was that he was meeting the last – now aged – generation of hilltop villagers – in the benign form of Quinto with his hunting dogs – and through him and the simple unearthed remains, Riccardo had felt some placemaking connection back to a time when the Roman landscape was abandoned in favour of the seemingly timeless one that he had grown up in and is today an iconic tract of Europe.

6

Breakfast with Colin Renfrew

Figure 6 Colin Renfrew on Kéros.

My friend Kostas said to me one evening this spring: 'Colin Renfrew is digging on [the island of] Kéros!! My friend, this is the dig of a lifetime. Go!' Kostas with uncharacteristic emotion was reacting to my news that Colin had invited me to see his new excavations in the dazzling heart of the Cyclades.

In all the years I have known Colin, I have never seen him in action in the field. I unwisely forsook the opportunity to dig at Phylakopi on Melos (the Cyclades) in 1975, choosing instead to chase potsherds in French museums. Likewise, I missed the chance to dig at (the megalithic tomb of) Quanterness in the Orkneys. These places along with Saliagos, Sitagroi, and Amorgos are tacit benchmarks of my life; places that have a special meaning simply because they are hefty, thought-provoking publications of a man whom I hold to be the greatest archaeologist of his generation. So, I accepted the invitation, and along with the Director of the British School at Athens, I embarked on an odyssey to Ano Koufoníssi, the Cycladic island nearest to Colin's new dig.

First stop Naxos by a propeller plane that glided out of the dark uncombed blue towards the Venetian castle, the *kastro*, before flopping onto an uncomfortably short runway with an airport building that resembles little more than a scruffy ticket office. Naxos boasts an old archaeological museum in the *kastro* with a collection of Cycladic figurines in polished wooden cabinets bettered only by those in the Goulandris collection in Athens. Better still, is the section of the Mycenean, Hellenistic, Roman and Byzantine town, excavated some years back by Olga Philaniotou, and now protected by a robust roof – rather reminiscent of an urban excavation in Denmark or Sweden. For those who advocate urban continuity from the Bronze Age until antiquity, few places in the Mediterranean illustrate it better.

From the centre of Naxos harbour sails an afternoon ferry, allegedly an express, connecting the smaller islands. It is crammed to the gunnels with cars, tackle and tourists and, like a Hebridean ferry, lifts and tumbles in the powerful swell. The boat beats its way through the white caps first to the spare little harbour of Iráklia, then eases into the awkwardly constricted harbour of Schinoússa, scene of a major police raid a month before when a villa was discovered to have underground stores with countless crates of looted antiquities. The finger of accusation was quickly pointed by the Greek press towards Sothebys in London and then Getty in Los Angeles. Global trafficking with its headquarters located here of all places seemed akin to a Hollywood film script – a few houses, casual boats bobbing in the ferry's wake and already a parched treeless landscape bathed by the cloudless Cycladic sky.

A little lighter now, the wind dropped, and the express set sail for Ano Koufoníssi, an island at the end of the chain, where Colin Renfrew was based in the oldest hotel. I indulged in some mellow reflection. Thirty-five years ago on a dark November night I sped through the Wiltshire countryside to the Corn Exchange in Devizes, having learned that this already remarkable man was lecturing on Stonehenge without Mycenae. Reading his early essays I was instantly seduced by the romance and epic quality of his scholarship. What was he like in person? As I opened the door, the Wiltshire Archaeological Society's AGM was nearing its completion, and immediately to my right was a ramrod erect, bespectacled man in a blue raincoat who turned and smiled courteously at me. He, it soon became clear, was the speaker. Ten minutes later, aided by slides, he set sail on his saga, bewitching the audience with elocutionary fireworks that, I suppose we must admit sadly, belong to another age. In many ways it was a Damascene experience as within six months Colin became my professor and, improbable as it might seem being a medievalist, a peerless mentor.

We waited in the hold, amongst heaps of cargo, as the ferry manoeuvred awkwardly against the bare pier. Then the back door lurched forward and in single file, tourists and natives alike, we advanced towards the evening sunshine. Tucked to one side, peering in, was a familiar beaming face, flat cap, blue tie and white shirt. He welcomed us and pushing his bicycle (brought from Cambridge), we ambled along the emptying waterfront as the ferry charged off into the opal seas towards Amorgos, mountainous in the shadowy distance.

We spent two days with Colin and Jane Renfrew and their team of twenty or so. This haven of whitewashed houses and picture-postcard windmills has already drifted from my memory. Colin has that effect. The briefing begins in the *apotheki*, the headquarters where finds are processed and drawings made. It would be improper for many reasons to describe the purpose and discoveries of his remarkable dig: only Colin could do it justice. Instead, I would like to recall the pleasure of Colin's stories and experience. He is regarded as a great theoretician and scientist who has instilled methodology in modern archaeology. There is, however, another Colin Renfrew. For over 40 years he has been working off and on surveying and excavating major archaeological sites.

More than four decades earlier Colin, then working on his doctorate at Cambridge, came upon the largely deserted islet of Kéros with its hillsides littered with figurine fragments and wove what he could into his pioneering account of the emergence of Neolithic in the Cyclades. Ten years on and this germ nourished his great book, *The Emergence of Civilization* (1972), known to his students as 'The Bible'. This book had a breadth and imaginative innovation that for a decade at least dominated research in Europe – not least mine – but, as Colin admitted over dinner on one of these Cycladic nights, was not particularly admired in the USA. Now, having recently won a prize, Colin thought why not invest these fortuitous riches in a project he had dreamed of doing for decades at Kéros.

Watching others run projects is always interesting. In Colin's case this was especially true. First, there is a genial military punctiliousness to the quotidian rhythm. Each part of the day, from the departure on the little fishing boat to the distant isle, is carefully and usefully regulated. Yet, far from being overbearing, the reverse is true. Responsibilities are delegated to just about everyone for one task or another. Everyone, within this framework, has a role, be it running a trench, sieving, working on a class of artefact or drawing. Colin inspected their trenches, but more to the point their notes and records as well, sharing the experience in all aspects of the project and winnowing out a collective narrative of the excavation. My impression was that everyone basked in this privileged benediction.

Even the workmen, young islanders who otherwise would be helping out in the seasonal bars and restaurants, were equally engaged in the enterprise. And no less caught up in the group ethic was Olga Philaniotou, the local inspector from Naxos newly promoted to be ephor of Mytilene, a multitude of islands away to the east. Olga explained to me that it was a life-changing decision to leave Naxos after more than a quarter-century, especially now she had the pleasure of working with Colin as his associate director.

The rhythm of each day was punctuated by breaks. Two were special: an ample loaf of fresh bread, cans of sardines, tomatoes and fruit for lunch: 'simple but very serviceable', Colin ventured. Much as we had taken lunch in the Biferno Valley survey in Italy in 1977, I observed – 'Ah, Graeme [Barker] (the Biferno Valley director and Colin's successor as professor of archaeology at Cambridge) was at Sitagroi with us in the '60s', Jane Renfrew intervened. Did

Graeme model his culinary programme on the master's? Then dinner with the team tucked around extended tables in a local taverna – they moved from one to another, sharing out their custom. Here, of course, Colin, past Master of Jesus College, Cambridge, was in his element. Everyone was welcomed, many with an apt question about the day's activities.

Over dinner – initiated with iced ouzo – the talk was of digs past and present controversies. Each of Colin's field projects has lasted about three seasons. The first, on the island of Saliagos near Poros, was shorter, and, it seemed, their favourite. Though a poor community (we did not talk about the discoveries, long since published), they had made enduring friendships, returning on occasions for weddings. Sitagroi in Thrace clearly had a special place too. He had sunk a huge, deep trench into this extraordinarily well preserved prehistoric tell encountering unique deposits with many Neolithic clay figurines. In retrospect, the scale of it seemed to surprise and delight him. Then there were expeditions to Melos and Amorgos, but when I asked about Orkney, Colin became lyrical with the memory. The project had grown out of the celebrated BBC 'Chronicle' films and his search to describe the impact of the radio-carbon revolution in rethinking the canonical interpretation of European prehistory as a project that diffused from the civilized orient to the barbaric north. The result is a majestic monograph, illustrated by masterful plans and sections of the megalithic monuments made by the Sheffield architect, Alec Dakin. But it was the Orcadian light and the poetry of its people that marked this experience.

Of course, we came to the unexpected police raid on the neighbouring island of Schinoússa where a villa packed with looted antiquities had come to light. The discovery led the police to check out another villa on the island of Paros and claim that a controversial ex-Getty curator possessed illegal antiquities. No-one much believed this. Tackling the scourge of looting has been championed by Colin, who appeared on a Greek television documentary about the local case. Over dinner, this elicited the news that Tom Hanks had a villa on one of the neighbouring islands and soon the Da Vinci Code star might be making a new film about the trafficking of antiquities.

Digging for Colin has been about people and places and above all their spirit. Perhaps this is why each of his fieldwork monographs encapsulates much more than the search to resolve a problem discretely using the most modern methodology. Rather like Mortimer Wheeler's great excavation reports, each is a chapter in an epic life.

We left on the 7.20 ferry almost an hour after Colin and his team set sail at dawn for their distant isle in its placid sea. Breakfast was simple but animated. What might be found today? What did this field of countless broken statuettes mean? Was there time to chase another intriguing lead? Greek coffee, honey, yoghurt and fresh bread, with Colin Renfrew already in full flow. He belongs to another age, his gifts and energy, his wisdom and grace, and above all his intelligence freely shared as we splash the viscid local honey this way and that.

His caique, having disembarked the team, was returning to harbour as our ferry departed, its craggy-faced captain saluting us with his klaxon. On the horizon I imagined Colin Renfrew, shaded by a wide-brimmed straw hat, leaning on his stick, gently bidding his young team to remove this or that. This has felt like a trip to an oracle, a privilege that easily eclipsed the magic of the Cycladic islands and their extraordinary prehistory.

7

Reviewing Lisa Fentress at Alatri

Figure 7 Lisa Fentress sampling mortar at San Sebastiano to date the monastery.

Lisa Fentress is a rare phenomenon these days. She is a distinguished practising archaeologist who has never held a permanent university post or managed an archaeological outfit, yet has a track record of published projects that would make most academics blush. I met her more than 25 years ago and was soon frequenting her kitchen table, off an intimate cortile filled with cats, close to Rome's Campo di Fiore. In the half-light of many a winter's evening, she and her husband, James – an expert on the mafia – generously hosted the waifs and strays passing through Rome's foreign schools and institutes. And either at this table or at their country house – a modestly refurbished convent in a deep-wooded Chianti-shire valley – provided the context (fuelled by good wine, of course) for meeting Italian colleagues whose methodologies seemed so alien to ours.

Lisa works with passion and zest: in English, French and Italian. Half measures do not exist for her. So with extraordinary self-discipline, she designs a project – in Algeria, Italy or Tunisia, finds a team, discovers bureaucratic hurdles because she has no university affiliation, overcomes the hurdles, excavates and surveys (has pitched battles with occasional individuals who take advantage of her generosity) and then heaves into action to produce major studies and monographs. So her *curriculum vitae* starts with her work on Roman North Africa and includes an important book on the Berbers. But it is in Italy that I have come to know her best. She made a field survey around the ancient Tuscan colony of Cosa, then excavated in Cosa itself. Both projects are gems, not least because in her spirited approach she challenges the *status quo* and attracts – as Mortimer Wheeler would have put it – 'damnation'. Without doubt, Wheeler would have admired her scholarship and personality, because each year brings new projects with new young students eager to learn on her digs, pilgrims at her kitchen table.

So I was happy to accept for review a copy of her latest monograph on the monastery of San Sebastiano at Alatri in southern Lazio. This project – mounted on petrol money alone with colleagues and fellows from the American Academy in Rome – falls right into my sphere of interest, a stone's throw from the Benedictine monastery of San Vincenzo al Volturno where I excavated for nearly two decades. I travelled with Lisa's handsome book for some months before falling ill and, needing distraction, I opened it. Naturally, I had assumed I should agree with Lisa. I was wrong.

Almost at once I was questioning her interpretation of the monastery. I put the book down, tried another, but was soon drawn back to Lisa's beguiling account. In a nutshell Lisa takes a solitary line of a late Roman writer to assert that San Sebastiano was founded in the fifth or sixth century in the era of St. Benedict (who founded nearby Monte Cassino). From this morsel of serendipity she weaves a story, taking each carefully described wall type in this bewilderingly rebuilt monastery to represent an historical episode. Walls are equated to a palimpsest of memories to confect a breathtakingly eloquent story. The bravura is admirable. The archaeological writing and analysis is peerless. But I reckoned it was wrong! The source, I believe, is inconsequential. Fifth- to sixth-century monasteries are essentially unknown in this part of Italy. Besides, the walls that she attributes to it look exactly like those well-dated at San Vincenzo two centuries later around AD 790.

So I procrastinated. Would the journal editor who sent me the book to review forget me? He did not. Eventually I sent my draft to Lisa and asked her to tell me what to do. Characteristically she replied with an avalanche of e-mails suggesting we visit San Sebastiano together, take some mortar samples for carbon 14 dating, and have a good lunch in a *ristorante* on the grand Samnite acropolis of Alatri, ancient *Aletrium*. Don't be seduced by her (arguments), the editor wrote, when I explained the situation . . .

We meet at Anagni, where she is currently excavating a second-century imperial palace. With scarcely a pause for reflection, she is telling me about her latest venture, then she is deconstructing the written text for San Sebastiano. Her mobile phone is buzzing and we career along as she drives one-handedly while excavating for it in her handbag. San Sebastiano lies 4 kilometres from the hilltop town of Alatri, 10 kilometres behind Frosinone, an industrial hub in southern Lazio. The last tract of the journey is made in sleeting rain.

The monastery sits on a spur overlooking the bowl of the valley, with the snow-covered hills rising up behind to form the wall of mountains which run south past Monte Cassino and north to Subiaco. Despite the dreary weather, the magnolia in the custodian's garden is blooming and he, too, seems delighted to see Lisa. He arms himself with a bunch of keys the size of candlesticks and we enter the seemingly deserted world of San Sebastiano.

In fact, as Lisa soon tells, it is not deserted. Sir John Leslie, an old friend of her father's, in whose Irish castle she stayed when she was a child, is the proprietor. Sir John is a beanpole of a man, approaching a century. He still visits the monastery each August and lives in the kind of Dickensian simplicity that is the stock of baronet living. His one indulgence is a painted nun, ghost-like on the far door of a dark corridor. The ghost, if I understood correctly, belongs to his Irish house and was painted here for nostalgia's sake.

The monastery has a glorious compactness to it, concealing two sheltered cloisters – an outer and inner one – within the towering walls that contain myriad phases of construction. Romanesque and thirteenth-century phases are plain to see, as the Clarissan nuns from Rome made the pre-existing house into a comfortable retreat. More evidence still is the work of the Renaissance humanist – Giovanni Tortelli (*c.* 1400–1466). He contributed a huge *loggia* (a gallery) to the fifteenth-century ensemble as well as two great staircases and of course, appropriate frescoes in the main chapel. Tortelli's interventions had their imitators too. In the 1930s, the penultimate proprietor, Romolo Giralico, used fragments of fake inscriptions and sculpture to feign phases that hinted of the Lombard and Romanesque ages. Even in the steady drizzle it is a gloriously intimate place, plainly full of history and memory.

So Lisa, ever the excited guide, provides a commentary on each wall. Now, though, a critical job must be done. Grasping a rusty hand-axe to drive her chisel into the mortar grouting of a distinctly curious wall, she prised out a matchbox size wad of cement and wrapped it in foil to send to the carbon 14 dating laboratory at Oxford. Each sample costs £1,000 to analyse, she says, as we wade through the sodden grass to the next testing-point. So, she has entered the tombola for a free date! One will do, she says chirpily, mindful of how she runs her digs: free accommodation, in this case with the ghostly nun in the baronet's fusty rooms; a little petrol money; and eager, willing, academicians.

San Sebastiano is a gem. Surrounded by olives, it towers over Alatri, itself one of the glories of the region – where stupendous cyclopean Samnite walls encased Hellenistic and Roman *Aletrium*, and where, we might presume a bishop looked up to the hilltop monastery. Was it founded in the age of St. Benedict, on the road south from Rome and Subiaco, towards the new spiritual hub of Monte Cassino? Or was it founded in the age of Charlemagne, as the celebrated but liminal area came to have new meaning for his new Europe, lying as it did on his politically vulnerable southernmost frontier?

Looking at the walls as Lisa chipped away with her chisel, I could not conceal my admiration for her gusto and enthusiasm, as well as her intellectual passion. But was I convinced?

I paid for lunch so, as I told Lisa, I could tell the commissioning editor of the review that I had not been bribed! Looking out from Alatri's acropolis, towards San Sebastiano, I understood why she was championing her version of the monastery's history. Indeed, I rather hoped the samples might provide an ambiguous date to permit us to pursue our amicable debate on future occasions.

8

With Giussy Nicolini where the Blue Begins

Figure 8 Thomas Ashby *c.* 1920 (courtesy of the British School at Rome).

Flying south of Agrigento the blue begins, even on All Saints Day. An Ionian light, it is the ravishing glory of the Middle Sea. I went to Lampedusa in the footsteps of Pope Francis and political grandees, conscious that this miniscule Italian outpost had borne a heavy burden as it grappled with the lives and accursed deaths of thousands of migrants. Here, over the past 30 years, tragedy has mixed with mass tourism to give Lampedusa a peculiar notoriety in Italy and abroad. I came to offer the help of our students. Could they contribute to writing grants, preparing programmes, and even running projects – shouldering a little of the island's burden? Speaking English, Italian and in some cases Arabic, might our students make a small contribution as Europe for the first time in two generations is challenged by a migration of biblical proportions? For our students, being embedded in the philanthropic front line might provide them with experience to engage in still greater challenges, because this migration is not set to cease soon.

As the propeller plane settled towards the airfield, the shadowy outline of Tunisia about 100 kilometres to the south became clear. Then bump, we were down, next to the kind of south Italian urban sprawl given free rein over the past 20 years. Being siesta time, the streets were empty, but the mayor was in her office. Giusy Nicolini has become a national figure, an articulate advocate for support for her people facing waves of impoverished, bewildered migrants from Libya. A self-confident woman who eagerly listens, she is not a natural politician, and is all the more fascinating for it. She is curious to hear how our university might help, but is not instinctively enthusiastic about promoting herself or her island's circumstances. Her primary problem is to combat the kind of corruption that has been endemic in Italy, and to improve the infrastructure on the island. But, then I mentioned the name of Thomas Ashby, my distant (legendary) forebear as Director of the British School at Rome – the first person to survey the archaeological remains on the Pelágie Islands (Lampedusa, Linosa and the uninhabited islet of Lampione) and the mayor's eyes beamed with delight. We debated which year he landed from *HMS Banshee* with the support of Rear Admiral Sir Assheton Curzon-Howe to make his survey – was it 1908 or 1910? – it was June 1909 – and then began to share stories based upon his report published a year later in the most obscure and arcane of annals. Now I must admit that anyone who admires Ashby wins my vote!

So to cut a long story short, Lampedusa has grown its tourism since the first airfield was constructed in the 1960s. Perversely, after Colonel Ghaddafi fired two scud missiles at the island's American base in 1986, tourism rocketed. Exact numbers of visitors to Lampedusa and its sister island, the extinct volcano of Linosa, appear to be vague. But there are roughly 70,000 beds offered by the island's 6,000 inhabitants, and as a result, the community is upwardly mobile, which, in Italy, means they have children. There are about 1,000 young Lampedusans. All of this is to the good. However, much of the construction has been unregulated, and managed with the kind of speculative eye that characterizes Andrea Camilleri's sardonic stories of the Sicilian Inspector Montalbano.

The mayor succeeded in obtaining piped water only two years ago, and many apartments are still not on the network. Her goal is to upgrade the island's facilities and in a moment I'll explain the benchmark in her mind. Confronting her is the island's reputation, largely from an incident in 2010 when 800 migrants were stranded for three winter months on Lampedusa's main street, the Via Roma. As became clear, such incidents no longer occur. The flotilla of coastguard vessels backed up by a legion of police on land and a discrete, state-of-the-art reception centre just outside the town have all but airbrushed the migrants out of the town's daily life. Forewarned by radar, the coastguard intercept the boats off shore and take their occupants to the reception centre – over 200 were brought ashore three days earlier – and swiftly, unlike absolutely anything else in Italy, these poor people are transferred to centres elsewhere in the country. The efficiency is dazzling. However, perhaps because it is dazzling in comparison to the norms of Italy no-one much wants to own up to the Lampedusa story!

So the mayor has another objective: to raise the bar on the island for tourists, add archaeology to the magic of its beaches. In her mind, she thinks archaeology might add lustre to her greatest achievement: in two words, Rabbit Island!

Surveyed first by William Henry Smith in 1814–1816 for the British Admiralty, this tiny offshore stack beside an arcing sandy beach where turtles nest was home to rabbits, hence its name. Anywhere else in Italy and rampant construction would have consumed this piece of paradise. Championed by Legaambiente, led by Giusy Nicolini, it is a swath of coastline worthy of the most majestic in Europe and often tops lists of the best beaches. It is sublime.

More than this it is an enduring index of how a champion can make a place and so contribute to its economic sustainability.

Now, add archaeology to the mix of island resources, and Lampedusa might increase the vacationing season, and with it the island's wider standing. The Soprintendenza at Agrigento are sympathetic, masterminding a new museum on the main street, the Via Roma, overlooking the new harbour. The talk is of the alarms, the electrics and winding staircase, then, with less assurance, of Lampedusa's treasures: Greek coins minted here with obverses depicting tuna, a statue dredged from the sea, Maltese Bronze Age farms, a late Roman cemetery and endless treasures secreted underwater. Like Rabbit Island, there needs to be a vision. Hence, the appeal of Thomas Ashby.

Ashby, an inveterate walker, surveyed the island over two days in 1909. He found the remains of Bronze Age huts like those he had helped excavate on Malta (presently the University of Malta is digging one of these on Lampedusa), and he reviewed the other remains belonging to a place that has attracted every quintessential Mediterranean interest: Punic, Greek, Roman, Byzantine, Arabic and, from recent times, the Bourbons. Lampedusa featured in the run-up to the Allied landings in 1943 when, codenamed Operation Corkscrew, British forces landed here in June of that year.

Two monuments are musts on any visit. Three kilometres west of the town beside the coast road is a sanctuary, a grotto with an elegantly whitewashed baroque façade. Dedicated to the Madonna of Porto Salvo, it is all that remains of a collection of cave dwellings occupying this south-facing canyon. The pivotal facility here is a decorated wellhead. Given Lampedusa's struggle with its water supply in recent times, it is important to note that Greek, Roman and later ships apparently berthed off-shore to take on sweet water from a network of Lampedusan wells like this.

The sanctuary has an important contemporary resonance: a sixteenth-century Italian slave, captured by the Ottomans, shipwrecked hereabouts, found salvation, so the story goes, thanks to the benign spirit of this place. The subject of a local pilgrimage each September, it is also believed to have had an Arabic history, co-existing for a time with the Christian deity, as was the norm on neighbouring Sicily from the tenth century onwards.

Further west, beyond the track leading to Rabbit Island, just off the road, the EU has supported the conservation of a traditional dry-stone farmhouse, the

Casa Teresa. A longhouse in all but name, its broad walls and flat roof belong to an Arab vernacular. In its ensemble of walled gardens is a reconstructed threshing floor, beyond which, occupying the far horizon, is the old American radar station, menaced by Libyan missiles in 1986. The restoration of this farmstead was only finished recently, but already bears the distressing hallmark of inattention; when we arrived, the only other visitors were two knaves in military drill illegally trapping finches.

So should the museum in Lampedusa's main street simply house the odds and ends so far found on the island? Here is the challenge. Rabbit Island is breathtakingly simple in its minimal but well-constructed paths, shaded spots and signage. Designed for visitors with a penetrating perceptiveness of the importance of the views, the crystalline blue sea and the fragility of the sands for nesting turtles, it is a tribute to twenty-first-century thinking. Shouldn't the new archaeological museum be as bold and forward thinking? The walls of the present Archivio Storico in the Via Roma, run by a charismatic enthusiast, Antonino Taranto, on behalf of an energetic local society, are covered with photographs, including Ashby's. This little treasure houses the endless stories that, in combination, make up the priceless history of this improbable place. All except one: that which has lent Lampedusa its notoriety and drew Pope Francis and politicians here – the migrants.

Modern Italy has learned to cope with this ghastly humanitarian crisis. All involved deserve our admiration, as they are learning and acting – perhaps for specific political expedience in some cases – to implement humane best practice. Now, surely the museum should be a portal not only to visiting places on these islands and finding pleasure in authentic treasures from the past, but also an opportunity to explain how the community has been shaped over time, confronting pirates, invasions and, of course, migration.

I did not meet or see one migrant, but I encountered an exceptional mayor in a place that is forever indelibly imprinted on my mind. As the plane thrust upwards and weaved around the massing storm clouds to pass over verdant volcanic Linosa, I could not get the sacred beauty of Rabbit Island out of my mind, and I harboured a secret and improper pleasure from my connection to Ashby, a truly great scholar who never wavered from faithfully recording the visceral conditions of people in places.

9

Remembering Albanian Heroines

Figure 9 Skënder Aliu, Iris Pojani and Vangjel Dimo and finds from the Devoll valley.

Liri Belishova was 20 when she joined the communist partisans in Albania and served as an heroic messenger from Party Secretary, Enver Hoxha, to his frontline troops, giving the go-ahead to take Tirana from the Germans in November 1944. Three years later, her husband, Nako Spiru, a founding member of the Communist Party and for two years its Minister of Economics was purged, leaving Liri a widow. For Hoxha, a pitiless and vengeful dictator, this was not enough. In 1960 Liri was sentenced to life in an internment camp, hard labour in the fields. For much of the next 31 years she was in Cerrik close to where the Devoll river meets the river Shkumbin in central Albania. Hardly an exceptional story from Hoxha's rule of terror, but when you pass through Cerrik you think of the starry-eyed Liri and her devotion to a cause and the mercilessness that proved it to be a chimera.

With his death in 1985, Hoxha left a land with a sub-Saharan economy, extreme poverty being the norm. In 1991 Albanians woke up to discover that they were at the bottom of the barrel, and in the 25 years since have struggled to keep pace with the world around them. A new generation urgently wants only to be European, to leave the anguish to history. This is the moment for investment and none is more propitious than the Devoll hydropower dam that, with a sister dam, will produce almost 20 per cent of Albania's electricity. Both projects are the brainchild of Statkraft, the Norwegian state power company.

How on earth did I end up in the Devoll valley and is it worth visiting? Well, like the Hollywood film-star, Michael Douglas, who once made this strange pilgrimage, I discovered a narrative that likely as not will bring an interesting future to the only Devoll town beyond Cerrik, Gramsh.

Gramsh lies in the foothills of the Vërça mountains. It is overshadowed by Mount Tomorr with a nimbus of snow in wintertime. Gramsh is where the Devoll hydropower project has based itself, bringing a strange cosmopolitanism to a world of shepherds and smallholders.

It was a phone call from Elenita Roshi who once skilfully managed the heritage projects at Butrint and Gjirokastra that lured me past Cerrik to the shadow of Tomorr. We spoke in late February. A serious problem needed solving. The new half billion euro dam was due to be plugged on 4 April, but one piece of paperwork was missing. The archaeology had been identified some years before but, due to misunderstandings, no assessment of the sites themselves had taken place. Now, the Norwegian company was keen not to imperil its global reputation by missing its deadline for plugging the dam. If the deadline were to be missed, the Albanian Government would be penalized for each lost day. So it was in the mutual interest of both parties to get the last piece of paper stamped by the end of March. For the company and the government the worst-case scenario was that the independent archaeological contractor would spin the work out to inflate their *per diem* price, and even worse, that a great discovery would ruin the tightest of timelines.

My task was simple: could I evaluate the work programme of the independent archaeological contractor, and assess the results to ensure the timeline was respected?

Albania has changed dramatically since first I came at the dawn of democracy in 1993. Mother Theresa airport – Enver Hoxha himself blocked the saint's return to Albania – is modern and efficient. There are good roads as far as Cerrik. Beyond, the roads are being upgraded as part of the dam's infrastructure. After heavy winter rain, crushed by the passage of heavy vehicles, travelling in anything less than a big SUV would be torture. The potholes and the maw of mud belong to a war zone. Life may be better than when this village housed forced labour camps, but everything is relative. Construction at the towering dam face itself was at full throttle. Massive modern equipment and a sense of urgency was evident everywhere. Such sights focused our thoughts on resolving the riddle of the Devoll valley's archaeology.

The valley is narrow and dark as it twists into a straight shot on being released from the high mountains. Roiling clouds darken the prospects in all directions: the territory looks unpropitious for much human history. A Bronze Age tumulus was excavated halfway up the valley when Hoxha was still alive. Near Drizë, close to a memorial erected to partisans executed in the Second World War, is a putative prehistoric cairn. More worrying for us, the survey carried out for the hydropower project identified a veil of small early classical sites running down the valley. Could any of these surface scatters of material turn into major monuments that might delay plugging the dam? Really everything depended upon the leadership of the contracted archaeologists.

Between a rock and a hard place, all the nervous stakeholders juggling gigantic forces knew that everything was at stake in this unlikeliest of archaeological projects. The finger pointed to the one person who commanded respect in the short time frame available. The daughter of a diplomat, Iris Pojani is Professor of Archaeology in the University of Tirana and an experienced field archaeologist. A specialist in ancient sculpture, she has excavated at all Albania's major sites. The Devoll project held no fear for her even though, with the late winter weather and the tight deadline, the task resembled the English reality TV show, *Time Team*.

On my first visit Iris and I inspected each of the so-called sites. None seemed terribly promising and set no alarm bells ringing in dam headquarters in Oslo. Quite the contrary, the poverty of the settlement history may explain why Gramsh was created here by the Hoxha regime, in part to terrace and work the rugged fastness. Today these hillsides are abandoned. A culture looking to extract every ounce of livelihood from this charmless terrain has come and gone leaving an extraordinary cultural landscape. Corrugated traces of terracing cover every angle to an extraordinary height. With the advent of democracy, this episode of inhuman farming ended as most of the workers fled to the capital, Tirana, or joined the millions of Albanians abroad. The command economy also aimed to dam the Devoll valley. Work began in the 1980s but stopped because of the dwindling spirit of the communist government.

Fast forward almost three weeks and I returned. Eight excavations were underway despite sleet and rain. Our visit to the first two was anything but easy. In a landrover lashed with mud we slipped and slid along a mule path that had all the ingredients of a road to the First World War trenches a century earlier. Leaving our vehicle we waded across a brook to visit a small collapsed Hellenistic dwelling. This simple household was deserted when the Romans brought Mediterranean prosperity to the Illyrian coastal plain. This miniature story was dwarfed by the deserted village 100 metres away where the brook met the Devoll river.

The mounds and rubble, on closer inspection, were all that remained of a village from the communist heyday. Judging from the battered fountainhead, there may first have been an Ottoman farm or hamlet here that was enlarged in the 1950s to include a school, a small *caserma* and other civic buildings. Called Darëzezë none of the buildings were in any way elaborate. Darëzezë fell victim to a forced removal of the community when a dam was first planned here in the 1980s. Its families were transported to a spot near ancient Apollonia close to the Adriatic Sea. Iris plans to speak to those surviving from this forgotten exodus. Being here made me think of Liri Belishova and her ordeal. Surely she knew the lost villagers and their struggle. Now in her nineties and living in Tirana, I wondered what she made of modern Albania, fashioned from its accursed histories.

On we walked past shepherds with thin sheep and growling mongrels. We followed riverside pastures covered, so Iris's trenches show, by the deep sediments washed down from the making of the terraces higher up. One trench contained Bronze and Iron Age sherds presumably swept down from a promontory positioned just above the high water line of the new dam. Pied wagtails and buzzards added an Arcadian charm to this stretch of our journey. Soon we were back in the landrovers and crossing the Devoll alongside fleets of earth-moving machinery preparing for the flood. Our next destination was the putative cairn by the monument to the resistance fighters. Trenches arced out in all directions but to no avail. Nothing prehistoric was found. In contrast, half a kilometre back along the valley, where we supposed traces of a Roman villa to be located, the trench archaeology is intriguing. Potsherds from a Hellenistic cemetery on the spur above have been driven down the hill and overlie more Iron Age and even earlier prehistoric sherds but no structures.

We made one last detour back across a causeway over the Devoll to the site of a riverside Bronze Age hut. Small as it is, it reveals the tenacious cultivation of niches in this dark valley trapped between the rich Korça plain 60 miles to the south-east and the great coastal littoral 60 miles to the west. With the imminent darkness we motored to Gramsh. Some believe the small town was named after the Sardinian communist philosopher, Antonio Gramsci (1891–1937), who traced his family's ancestry to the Albanian exiles who settled in Italy (known as the Arbëreshë). Whether apocryphal or not, the town square retains an understated socialist dignity with the municipality on one side and an appropriate large museum opposite.

When, on my first visit, we entered the museum, it was as though we had freed the air of ages. Musty and dusty, the ethnographic treasures and fuzzy glass cases full of small finds from local digs were badly in need of some love. Once this museum served Gramsh, to provide its citizens with origin myths.

This no longer being the case, Iris prudently commandeered it for washing, sorting, marking and documenting finds from the trenches. Her young team, overseen by experienced archaeological stalwarts, Skënder Aliu and Vangjel Dimo, had done wonders. Order had been put into the material, a narrative emerging as if by magic.

The Devoll valley was never rich but it attracted later prehistoric and Hellenistic smallholdings. With the gravitational pull of Roman cities on the coast as well as along the Via Egnatia that bisected Albania from Dyhrrachium (modern Durrës) running to Constantinople (modern Istanbul), the valley was abandoned. The washed and marked finds in Gramsh museum contained virtually nothing of the mid-to-late Roman era or, for that matter, from the Medieval or even Ottoman eras. How much has been obscured by the huge land-moving exercises of Communist times is not entirely clear. One story is obvious to us all, now Statkraft has successfully plugged the dam, and, with the thawing snows, this spring the mountain water is rising each day.

More than electricity has been produced by the hydropower project. On the company's behalf, Iris's archaeological campaign shows that this valley was a backwater until Gramsh itself assumed its modern shape. From the 1950s its primary purpose was to produce Kalashnikovs in a suitably anonymous place unknown to most Albanians. The bullets were made elsewhere. Michael Douglas visited the Kalashnikov factory in 2000 to encourage the surrender of stolen weapons. This brick-built socialist 'cathedral' lies on the edge of Gramsh, dwarfing every house old and new. Forgotten now perhaps, but immensely important for future generations when Gramsh becomes a waterside town and a centre for trekking and watersports. With the history of settlement culminating in the new dam (at the second attempt), Gramsh can turn its intended anonymity to advantage. This new narrative has surely to combine watersports with the millennial conquest of the marginal, including, of course, the story of forced labour by heroines like Liri Belishova.

Finding the Senses

Hearing

10

Boreal Butrint and its Golden Oriels

Figure 10 Eternal Butrint: looking towards the Straits of Corfu (courtesy the Butrint Foundation).

Butrint (ancient *Buthrotum*) is eternal. It owes a priceless debt to Virgil who in *Aeneid* had his exiled hero from Troy, Aeneas, pause here on the way to found Rome. At a stroke, Butrint was on the world map! Virgil's choice of Butrint – 'a Troy in miniature' – was no accident. A member of Augustus's new imperial court at Rome, he was paying personal tribute to Augustus's right-hand man, Agrippa, whose first wife came from Butrint. With such serendipity this place has been forever sealed in aspic, at least until our era! For most visitors today, however, Butrint conjures up an entirely different experience. It is the Other, a paradise, a place in a Homeric landscape, somewhere simply and pleasantly timeless. It was extraordinarily beautiful when Enver Hoxha's infernal regime collapsed in 1991, quite unforgettable when I first ventured here in 1993, and remains a precious oasis within the mayhem of modern Albania today. Returning to visit the new excavations, the glorious assault on one's senses is as powerful as ever. You need know nothing about Aeneas to be seduced by the shimmering reflections off the lagoon, or to fall in love with the shafts of sparkling light on the monuments filtered by the woodland canopy where golden oriels flit through the foliage, grumbling like tropical parrots. Butrint really fits our new global ideals of a UNESCO world heritage site (it was inscribed in 1992).

On a mission

I came first at the suggestion of the British ambassador in Rome. Lord Rothschild and his friend Lord Sainsbury were seeking an archaeologist to dig here. Together, the lords had created a foundation after briefly visiting this erstwhile pariah state. As for me, I had always wanted to excavate a classical port on the Mediterranean: being at the crossroads of the *Mare Nostrum* this promised to be the opportunity of a lifetime. Then reality intruded. The barely dressed children dancing with their mutts around the plane when it landed in Albania's capital, Tirana, illustrated what lay ahead: a land benighted by 50 years of impoverishment presented to a slave nation as paradise on earth. Ravaged by the parched-earth destruction of olive groves, vineyards and collective farms by its starving peasants as the tyrants fell, it was like visiting a film set on location at the end of World War II. Every encounter was a shrill lament about the loss of opportunity, the searing victimization of the decent, and profound fear of the future. With the mention of Butrint, though, there was a visible counter-reaction – Butrint equalled paradise on earth. The first to make this point to me, as chance had it, was the first Albanian I encountered a mere three hours after arriving: Prime Minister Aleksänder Meksi. Finding him was a kind of puzzle. No-one stopped us entering the tawdry, Italianate government building, so we marched resolutely on straightening our ties until beyond the last door in this labyrinth we discovered one of Albania's previously well-known archaeologists. He described the calamity of his country but on reaching the point of the meeting, Butrint, he switched gears, becoming unexpectedly lyrical. This was more than an archaeological site that he was offering me, this was paradise. There were almost tears in his tired eyes. It was as though he was negotiating the hand of his daughter – something precious beyond words. So often afterwards I sensed, when the hellishness of working in Albania had become too great, this belief in the virginal property of this spiritually exceptional place came to the fore. How could you fail such a maiden was the unspoken question? Twenty years have passed and daily life has mellowed. Albania has prospered despite its arrantly corrupt governments. Amusingly, Albania's premier treasure today is where brides parade in their gowns with silken trails like flocks of long-tailed swallows once summer has come. After 20 years, the sylvan spirit of Butrint, in contrast to so much of Albania, needlessly forfeited to craven development, is as magical as ever. Let me try to explain how this miracle (of preservation) happened.

On first seeing Butrint on a misty September morning, I grasped the meaning of Prime Minister Meksi's unexpected lyricism. Butrint, in its lakeland setting, owns a Homeric landscape. Here, as Lawrence Durrell remarks, 'the blue really begins': the Ionian light grades blues, and the perpetually choppy waters of the Straits of Corfu invest even more colour in this unforgettable seascape. It was obvious that the Butrint Foundation, during its watch, must prioritize protection of this place for future visitors while bringing new archaeological thinking to this wonderfully time-warped place.

But this idyll was fragile. Cutthroat paladins circled Butrint in those first years, and still do. Marinas, golf courses, helicopter pads and much besides were promised so that the concrete desolation on this coast might resemble the tragic anonymity of Corfu. Our resistance was valiant and idealistic – denounced in one archaeological congress in the palace of ministers as tourism archaeology – until our chance arose when a brief civil war in 1997 plunged Albania into chaos. Now off limits to tourists, backed by the Getty Conservation Program, UNESCO and the World Bank, in April 1998 we mounted a management plan workshop to create a park at Butrint, and with persistence we contrived the making of a much enlarged world heritage area (encompassing the buffer zone around the site) in 1999. Then, working with the prescient minister of culture, Edi Rama, supported by the supreme and steadfast benevolence of the Packard Humanities Institute, we created a Butrint-based administration that along with new boundaries and strategic plans were up and running by 2000. Notwithstanding years of corruption and a rollercoaster ride of ups and downs, 13 years later this park is here to stay, a perceived model in Albania. Park director Raimond Kola expects 100,000 visitors a year to pass through the electronic ticket gates, keeping 20 or more people in work and, through seasonal projects, many more local workers besides.

A liminal place

Until 1990, a visa was needed to pass the customs post just south of Saranda. The narrow coastal road was created for the visit of Nikita Khrushchev in May 1959. Until then, archaeologists and a few bold visitors came by boat. This liminality protected the archaeological site from the wanton destruction around Corfu's once exceptional coastline. Self-selecting visitors to Butrint were greeted as I was in 1993 by a sylvan paradise that had barely altered in decades. Khrushchev, as it happens, was no admirer of old things. He moaned about the smell of dead vipers (all beaten to death in advance of his visit) and menacingly muttered that from here a submarine base might destroy the West. His hosts, though, grasped the magical properties of Butrint and cautiously conserved its monuments, letting the spirit of the place speak for itself. Digs by the Albanian Institute of Archaeology modestly advanced the great excavation campaigns of Luigi Maria Ugolini, made between 1928 and 1936. Ugolini, being a Fascist party member, could only be feted cautiously by his communist successors. So they removed his statue in an act of damnation, but excavated to affirm his interpretation of the city's 3,000-year history.

Ugolini had first visited Butrint in 1924, drawn to it by Virgil's description and the contrasting accounts of two spies (on opposite sides) during the Napoleonic wars, William Martin Leake and François Pouqueville. The prominent Roman and Medieval (as opposed to Greek) remains initially put him off, as did its remoteness. Finding any remains of the town visited by the exiled Trojans appeared to be unlikely. However, Ugolini had an eye for an opportunity. In 1928, with the bi-millennial celebrations of Virgil on the horizon, he returned; within weeks he had found the Hellenistic theatre. Using armies of workmen and railway wagons he excavated on a Schliemann-like scale at Troy and provided visitors retracing Aeneas's wanderings on a bi-millennial cruise with a magnificent new chapter for the archaeology of Aeneas (none of which, I should carpingly note, actually belonged to the age of Aeneas). However, Ugolini's cruise-ship tourists, like today's visitors, did not mind this minor anomaly.

Dave Hernandez's dig

When we began our excavations we naturally turned to Ugolini's reports, dedicated to Mussolini, as well as those by his successors, tacitly dedicated to Enver Hoxha. Over a dozen seasons, we had the good fortune to excavate in just about every part of Butrint, developing a twenty-first-century picture of its many histories. In numerous publications I have given a flavour of these discoveries. For this summer's visit, though, I am here to see the excavations by Dave Hernandez from Notre Dame University. Dave is fashioning a new, important chapter that builds upon the work of his fascist, communist and Butrint Foundation predecessors.

Dave began digging with me at Butrint in 2003. In his first week he nearly decapitated one of his fellow diggers. Worse than the head-wound was a visit to Saranda hospital! The digger survived, thankfully, swathed in thick bandages like a cartoon character, while Dave not only learned how to swing a long-handled shovel but also how to become a talented archaeologist. Ten years on, now a professor of classics, he is completing an excavation that exceeds Ugolini's in both scale and ambition. Tall, lean and powerfully focused, he learnt Albanian as a Fulbright Fellow to Tirana. He has used it to great advantage to motivate his workmen to not only dig deeper than anyone before him, but also to train local lads to draw and record. Dave began his project at the forum of Butrint in 2005; he wrote his doctorate on the first excavations then, after exploring other sites in Albania, he returned to unleash three blockbuster seasons. His devoted team not only found the Roman forum pavement and the well-preserved ensemble of civic monumental buildings around it, but dug deeper to push below the Hellenistic agora. Deeper, he urged them, using buckets, pumps and vim! Seven metres deep, his team excavated like Dickensian mud-larks, until below the waterlogged Archaic Greek levels they struck . . . oil! The story of the forum encompasses 2,000 years, exactingly pealed away layer by layer, much of it discovered in a viscous muddy water expelling a mild sulphurous menace. With the promise of a new trail through these excavations, once conserved, Butrint will add more monuments to its already impressive portfolio.

Dave's excavations hold a wonderful fascination for me. First, I am 'excited', as they say in America, to take pleasure in his brilliant management of his team and the archaeology to construct a new story. The new discoveries keep Butrint firmly in the news, indubitably helping to protect and promote it. Second, the afterlife of the Roman forum is exceptional. Seldom have ancient civic centres merited careful examination. In Butrint's case, the story shows how much must have been lost in comparable Mediterranean towns.

In these new excavations the pavement of the forum, almost as pristine as the day it was laid two millennia ago, has been wantonly ripped apart first by an earthquake in the 360s. This was followed a decade later by a 'sea wave' – a tsunami – as described by Cedrenus, which overwhelmed Epirus. Either seismic catastrophe might explain the dramatic change in land-sea levels. Responding to this calamity, Butrint's grandest fifth-century buildings were constructed on elevated terraces burying (and therefore protecting) the forum pavement. Was this the same earthquake that sank Roman Venice at the head of the Adriatic Sea? If so, Dave's dig contains certain and vivid evidence of its fury. Here, too, he has found the now inimitable traces of ancient Butrint's undignified demise: an untidy scatter of sixth-century graves dotted in and out of the desolate buildings marking the end of a millennium of extra-mural burial of the dead. This left a handful of doughty citizens in what one Byzantine historian later described as 'mouseholes'. One such mousehole was a modest stone hall found in these excavations, grand by Dark Age standards, dismissive by classical comparenda. Far more impressive, clinging high above the treacherous waterlogged areas of Butrint, Dave has uncovered a line of new, purpose-built dwellings. It's as though an early eleventh-century (Byzantine) Augustus intentionally re-invigorated civic life, safe from flooding. These mid-Byzantine two-storey dwellings brought a mercantile grandeur back to Butrint, and undoubtedly coincide with a powerful renewal of the town's fortifications. Another telling index of this significant urban moment is a long boundary wall, separating the properties in much the same way that tenements in English towns like Winchester and York were being fixed at this same time. Massive in purpose, this urban renewal was short-lived. A fine town-house replaced it only to perish in a conflagration in the later fourteenth century as the Venetians took possession of Butrint, and made it Corfu's 'protector and right eye'. At this point the old civic centre was finally eviscerated. Butrint was reduced to a fortress to defend the fishing grounds; the woodlands, now majestic by any standards, cloak the lower terraces of the acropolis where Dave has focused his operations.

Dave Hernandez's dig complements our efforts to fashion a Mediterranean story from numerous excavations dotted both inside and outside the ancient town. Together, we have brought modern archaeology to Albania, trained armies of students, and forcibly adjusted Enver Hoxha's isolationist history to the geo-politics of the Greek, Roman, Byzantine, Venetian, and Ottoman worlds, just as its modern visitors belong to a larger global picture.

Wandering beyond the dig on this sunlit morning I find all manner of visitors. A French team are re-examining our studies of the sixth-century baptistery with its extraordinary mosaic pavement. With them are members of Albania's Institute of Monuments giving the pavement its annual check-up (pursuing the programme we instigated a decade ago). Following the woodland path made for Khrushchev's visit, I arrive first at the Great Basilica, then veer off along the lakeside fortifications, newly conserved by a Butrint Foundation team. On beyond, a group of Albanian schoolchildren are gathered around the colourful site panel directing them to the Hellenistic hill fort of Kalivo in the hazy distance, and to the villa associated with the Pomponii family that we excavated on the lakeshore at Diaporit. From here, the darkened path threads through the Lion Gate where an Archaic temple tympaneum has been reused as a lintel in a Byzantine postern gate.

Further up a team is now clearing the vegetation covering the extra-mural Roman cemetery. On and upwards to the acropolis, where members of Dave's team are quietly processing the crates of finds unearthed by the mudlarks. Pots are washed, labelled, boxed and prepared for the specialists. Meanwhile, rake-thin, Michael McKinnon from the University of Winnipeg, Canada is measuring, logging and muttering admiring comments about the animal bones from the forum trenches. From here can be heard the echo of the throng of visitors around the theatre far below. Soon, in their hundreds, panting after the lengthy climb to the acropolis with its achingly beautiful views, they pause to take photographs and then peep into the museum, nestling in the bowels of a 1930s castle worthy of a Hollywood movie. The Butrint Foundation refurbished the museum in 2005. A labour of love, inspired by the then Director of the Foundation, Danny Renton, many say it's the best museum in Albania. Certainly, it honours the pledge made years before to Prime Minister Meksi. Paying homage to a long history in text, photographs, reconstructions, statues and small objects, it conveys exactly how the 100,000 tourists, brides included, see it: a glorious confection of Mediterranean history in a seemingly timeless landscape between the Ionian Sea and the Epirote mountains overlooking Lake Butrint.

Butrint is a happy place: an island paradise dedicated to the past but articulated now for the voracious appetite of visitors who want to take pleasure in a lost world. To help them, of course, there is a restaurant conveniently to hand, the Livia. As in ancient and Medieval times, there is prize fish – *cozze*, not to be missed – as well as mussels. Remind yourself over lunch that batty Venetian fishermen defended this Balkan enclave for 400 years, three times against massive Ottoman armies, for the sake of these aquatic creatures. Once eaten, never forgotten.

Looking back over 20 years of Albanian adventures, many thoughts come to mind. First and foremost is the heady tenacity of the pioneers of our project. They/we knew it mattered. It did; today you can take pleasure in the wealth and status the park has brought to this little country. Such is its success, the grumbling golden oriels in all their luminous finery, like the cumbersome pelicans visiting the lake beyond, go unnoticed. Above all, we made certain that Butrint continues to be magical. Whether Aeneas actually came here or was merely a fictive piece of imperial propaganda makes not a jot of difference. What really matters is the presentation of this Mediterranean story and the sustained conservation of the excavated areas that are second to nowhere south of the Alps. Many places tell a Greek or Roman story, or even a Medieval one. None colourfully span all these millennia taking in the whacky tales of its champions, its archaeological placemakers.

Butrint is a world heritage site that works. It is the legacy of the Butrint Foundation – of Jacob Rothschild and John Sainsbury – a place that defies the twenty-first-century imagination yet, thankfully, is an established part of it.

11

Sublimity: Hidden in the Togate's Folds

Figure 11 Struggling to land a togate statue at Butrint.

Butrint (ancient *Buthrotum*) in Albania has, over time, produced a good deal of trophy art, as some call it! Our project, however, has singularly failed to find any. Indeed, we have smiled politely and with extreme earnestness applied ourselves to the intellectual rigours of understanding the long history of this idyllic Adriatic port. So, we have bombarded the place with every intellectual weapon in our modern armoury. Our reward, without doubt, has been the fascination of appreciating that our tale is, indeed, helping to rewrite the history not only of this place, but also of the region. And yet ... every visitor asks: 'Where did Luigi Maria Ugolini find all those statues?' closely followed by

'And have you found any?' (the latter question meaning: how come he could do it [and die at 41 with the comforting knowledge of his achievement] and you cannot?).

Underlying this, of course, is the whole business of politically correct archaeology. Searching for trophy art, let me remind you, is politically incorrect unless you are chasing something taught to every university undergraduate today as [post-] post-processual/cognitive archaeology.

Now, I can provide a very good reason for our new excavations in the heart of Butrint. Not least, we have set up an interesting hypothesis about the Roman colonization of Butrint and its great Asclepian sanctuary under first Julius Caesar then Augustus after the battle of Actium in 31 BC, based upon a large excavation in the city's suburb. How did the hypothesis square with what was happening in the heart of the town? More to the point, where was the forum, the civic centre of the colony?

Well after a month we found the forum with its pristine pavement made of well-cut slabs (a magic moment) and in an abandoned drain off to one side, we found a full-size statue. At first we exposed only its sandalled foot. Days later I was telephoned by a journalist to enquire how it was that I had excavated the first Roman leather sandals in Butrint! It seems that a report of the discovery of the marble figure had been mangled in the telling.

But the magic moment of the season was not in the full exposure of this headless figure with his flowing toga in Pentelic marble, but in the removal of this tonne of marble from its constricted resting place in a drain little wider than the statue itself, down a trench more than two metres deep.

As in the way of Mediterranean archaeology, a colleague arrived at midday and said 'we'll pluck it out now' . . .

'NOT NOW?' I ventured nervously, conscious of a team around me who had fallen deeply in love with this mid-second-century headless patrician. My mind flashed back to a similar incident when I was a student supervising a dig in Turkey and my foreman browbeat me into shifting a column twice his height. What remains etched in my memory is his creased smiling face consumed with terror as the column juddered a fraction off crushing him. So, I argued fiercely with my colleague, urging him to find Kiço, Butrint's all-purpose factotum, a veritable expert at moving everything (legally and illegally).

As in the way of such debates, I was told Kiço was in Greece. 'Greece? I exclaimed, 'he was here yesterday ...' Of course, he was only three kilometres away, but my colleague felt that now was good statue-moving weather. Still, applying firm judgement (i.e. I was overly robust in pressing my point), we postponed the lifting operation until Kiço was available at midday the next day.

Kiço duly arrived with his rusty tripod and every able-bodied man he could find, plus some polystyrene. The task was simple. The statue needed to be raised up three metres and then rolled out a further three metres to the pathway where, wrapped in polystyrene for protection, it could be then hauled onto a vehicle. Simple really. And so it proved.

Kiço commanded quietly and my Albanian colleagues obeyed. One leg of the tripod was held down awkwardly by the two largest workmen, who were delighted to win their role. Then Kiço eased a frayed woven belt around the togate statue. Tugging the old communist pulley, the statue levitated into the air. Kiço quietly instructed his team of ten and, before long, the statue was balancing on the polystyrene on the adjacent wall, released from the drain after 1,800 years.

Then, a very Butrint moment occurred. Kiço yelled uncharacteristically and the word went up ... snake. Harboured in the lower folds of the toga had been a viper. It could never have suspected the unexpected turn of events which led to Kiço madly dancing a jig in the confined space, grabbing a shovel, and destroying the creature in a fitful frenzy. It brought to mind the account of how, when Nikita Khruschchev visited Butrint in May 1959, the Albanian dictator, Enver Hoxha had armies of beaters seeking and destroying the snakes in case one might bite the Soviet leader. The mangled corpses were strung up as prizes to garner his gratitude. Instead, allegedly dismayed by the fetid smell, Khrushchev damned the Albanians.

Next, our statue was swung onto a steep, angled barrow run, placed before the trench end. Its elegantly carved folds now shapely clear to all for the first time. Sublimity: the nano-second sound of ecstacy, of an unalloyed expression of massed joy. Everyone, emerging from everywhere, was suddenly in on the event – pushing, pulling the togate figure up. Along with the workmen there was the Vice-Director of the Institute of Archaeology, his straw trilby slightly cocked as he pushed; there was our driver, who had heard the ruckus and joined in, the mangled tattoos on his arms pumping at the plinth; in there heaving too was the smartly dressed local tourist agent, who was passing with 50 or more sweating Germans. Kiço calmly commanded them all and for five minutes, like an old-fashioned village tug-of-war, the marble statue resisted until the combination of forces all mucking in together beached the handsome creature on the pathway. All the time, the excavators marvelled, hearts in their mouths, while the lines of German onlookers loudly entreated us to get out the way as digital flashes illuminated the ensemble in the midday sun. Then, in an instant, it was over and, bound in the frayed ties, the togate was removed. Today it sits proudly on its own plinth in the atrium of Butrint's new museum.

Headless, in his patrician dress, posed nonchalantly as if holding a book scroll and about to march off, he was doubtless a person of consequence. Our specialist in sculpture, Inge Lyse Hansen, thinks his dress is more Greek than Roman and points to similar second-century statues from the nymphaeum of Annia Regilla and Herodes Atticus at Olympia. We can only wonder what happened to his head when the body was discarded in a drain. Today, ripped from his secret drain, this anonymous celebrity stands silently in his new home, an observer, no longer a participant in our excavation. Truth be told, he seems forlorn after such excitement, but, then, trophy art is, I always explain, nowhere near as exciting as the fleeting sense when we encounter the past, engaging and even hearing its magic.

12

Fireworks at Copán

Figure 12 The author with the Honduran archaeologist, Ricardo Agurcia, at Copán, 2011 (courtesy Kate Quinn).

I tend to sum countries up by how they treat their archaeological sites and, in common with everyone I know, their airport security. On these grounds, Honduras, one of the world's poorest countries, is a world-leader. Its only UNESCO World Heritage Site, inscribed in 1980, is the great Mayan capital of Copán, close to the Guatemalan border. Magnificently maintained and presented, this is quintessentially what a world-class site should be – awe-inspiring archaeology in an unforgettable location.

My visit was occasioned by a meeting to arrange an exhibition featuring the spectacular finds from the 1990s acropolis excavations to be mounted in the Penn Museum: *Maya.2012: Lords of Time*. This exhibition centres upon a reading of the Mayan calendar – hieroglyphs read by only a few experts – which some believe predicted the end of the world on 23 December 2012. The museum has adopted this anticipated catastrophe in order to add an apocalyptical overlay about how, in recent times, the Maya glyphs were cracked to tell a new tumultuous history of their kings and queens. The Terrible Tudors pale by comparison. Their own apocalypse, judging from these excavations, came suddenly in the so-called Late Classic, the AD 820s or so, when the dynasty fell suddenly, and Copán remained interred in a dark jungle until the redoubtable Frederick Catherwood and John Lloyd Stephens discovered it in 1845. From the pinnacle of the acropolis, clumps of this jungle run away to the east, but in truth, this place has been sprung from the heart of darkness. Its mown, grassy lawns now covering the erstwhile white plastered plaza are worthy of a cricket ground, while glistening ageless saber trees with their web of roots grace the shoulders of the ruins like stately sculptures.

Copán is essentially a monumental civic centre arranged around a great plaza and attached ballcourt, surrounded by the great compounds of its aristocrats. The acropolis on one side of the plaza is a pyramid that, like a wedding cake, grew incrementally with the vainglorious ambitions of each Copán king. Almost every king entombed the grandiosity of his predecessor, leaving the form and mausolea of his forebears buried beneath a palimpsest of superimposed stepped structures.

Bordering the ballcourt is temple 26, dominated by the hieroglyphic stairway. The quintessential expression of jungle folly, it is exquisitely carved, the 1,250 glyph blocks telling the epic story of Copán's kings, with the spirit of a stairway leading steeply upwards to the heavens. Only 50 years ago, a Penn researcher, Tatiana Proskouriakoff, played a critical part in cracking the glyph code. The stairway was started by Waxaklajun Ubaah K'awil (18 Rabbit), the thirteenth ruler who after a reign of 43 years was captured and executed on 3 May AD 738 by the king of the neighbouring city of Quiriguá. After an uneasy interval, it was completed by K'ak' Yipyaj Chan Kawil 1 (Smoke Shell Squirrel), the fifteenth ruler, in AD 755. Now conserved and carefully recorded by Barbara Fash from Harvard University, it belongs to those few iconic man-made wonders of the world from the sphinx to the Colosseum in Rome to the library of Celsius at Ephesus and in modern times, the Empire State building.

The plastic sculptures and glyphs of the stairway are not exceptional: Copán clearly celebrated its sculptors. Apart from the stele the size of Easter Island statues carved to patterns worthy of the Irish high crosses, there are countless elements, decorated stone blocks that once formed massive mosaic façades, worthy of the baroque era.

The glyphs on the stairway tell of earlier kings, something that Mayan archaeologists hotly debated. Some believed the glyphs; some didn't. This led to the 1990s Acropolis project being featured in the Penn exhibition. The universities of Harvard, Pennsylvania and Tulane collaborated to penetrate the mass of the acropolis at different levels in search of earlier iterations of the pyramids and the tombs of their benefactor monarchs. Loa Traxler, who assisted Bob Sharer from Penn in excavating the earliest levels of the royal centre, was my guide in the Penn tunnel, starting midway up the east side of the acropolis. Closed to the public as yet, this person-sized passageway was burrowed along the visible lines of earlier terraces. The tunnel then twisted and turned around features belonging to an earlier temple until it reached a ruddy-coloured plastered relief that betokened the façade of an earlier temple with glyphs that ascribe it to Ruler 2 and a date, AD 437. The excitement, Loa recalled, of discovering this was nothing compared to zig-zagging downwards into the vaulted chamber below, known as the Hunal Tomb. Breaking into it, Bob and Loa found the remains of an elderly man with notched and jade inlaid teeth, graced by a warrior's headdress – a shell helmet – and accompanied by numerous objects including a deer effigy vessel containing cacao (chocolate). The man, they deduced, confounding the sceptics, was K'inich Yax K'uk' Mo' (Great-Sun First Quentzal Macaw), the founding king of Copán from AD 426–437.

The humidity here is intense, but Loa urged me onwards ever deeper into this temple. For her, the prize discovery was another vaulted mausoleum known as the Margarita Tomb which contained unprecedented riches. On one side a step with a glyph mentions the first two rulers, but the body whose bones were painted with cinnabar was that of a great lady, almost certainly the wife of K'inich' Yax K'uk' Mo'. Her tomb was the most elaborate and richly furnished of any at Copán: multiple jade and shell necklaces, dozens of polychrome painted pots, mirrors, rings, and textiles.

At a level above, Ricardo Agurcia, the founder and president of the Copán Foundation, former director of the Honduran Institute of Archaeology and key collaborator in the Acropolis project, proudly led me into his tunnels high above the Hunal and Margaritas tombs. Being tall and lean, Ricardo's tunnels are spacious, mined in for perhaps 30 metres. At different points these veered inwards to discover the so-called Rosalila Structure: a magnificent ornamented temple entirely entombed within the later pyramid. Dating to the mid-sixth century, the entirely smooth plastered exterior is gorgeously painted with red ochre, some details being in bright green, yellow and orange. Ricardo's team had to engineer a massive space to reveal its intricate cosmological glory. Like an illuminated manuscript, it conveys compelling messages, centring on K'inich Ahau, the Sun God and the spiritual founder of the Copán dynasty, K'inich Yax K'uk' Mo'. Its second level, dominated by burlesque masks of a monster, pays tribute to the birthplace of maize. Winding around the darkened chambers, we arrived at the uppermost level where a smoking skull serves as an incense burner. This showy sacred monument is reconstructed in all its blazing colours as the centrepiece of the sculpture museum, created by Ricardo and his colleagues at the entrance to the park. Few excavations have made such a deep impression upon me: the skilful logic of the enquiry was rewarded by a peerless discovery, both majestic in form and accompanied by spectacular ritual objects.

These great excavations, publicized by *National Geographic* in the 1990s, prompted the interest of thousands of tourists. About 140,000 make the journey here each year. These numbers in turn helped the government's Institute of Anthropology and the Copán Foundation to protect and present the archaeological site. The glades are meticulously maintained by a cohort of over 60 workmen. Then, quite unexpected, there is the added attraction of the scarlet macaws. Several flightless pairs of Honduras's dazzling national bird greet visitors at the ticket office, begging tidbits like feisty cockerels. This July, though, the park carefully released five flying pairs into the woods. Like Chinese fireworks, streaks of fiery blue and red, these birds, cawing raucously, strike a sparkling parabola from the high woodland canopies to thrill the audience in the plaza. More will soon be released to join the parrots in making a cacophony of jubilant song, eclipsing the pedestrian efforts of the site guides who hoot to illustrate the acoustic properties of the plaza.

Mention must also be made of two other matters. Close by is the research centre where we held our meeting. This includes not only laboratories for the archaeologists but a warehouse for thousands of sculptures, amassed to make a corpus that includes the glyphs constituting a precious royal archive. Few sites worldwide dignify their collections so wonderfully well. No less impressive are the services of the little town of Copán Ruinas. Six thousand people live here, served by a flotilla of red tricycle taxis. These doggedly bump over the uneven cobbled streets, ferrying visitors to a whitewashed fortress on the hilltop housing an intelligently arranged children's museum as well as to the 28 estimable hotels and equally satisfying eateries including Twisted Tanya's and Jim's Pizza.

Copán is the apogee of the World Heritage brand, a place that, in essence, is the metaphorical capital of Honduras. Thanks in particular to the assiduous efforts of the Copán Foundation, a Honduran NGO, nothing about the experience here is tawdry. UNESCO could learn so much from the efforts of the local champions who have made the great history and archaeology of this place work to effect employment for those in the region. In this sense, the Maya have never died. Harnessed to the rhythmic sounds of the jungle, and the eerily frenzied cawing of scarlet macaws in free flight, this is a place to treasure. Passing through security in San Pedro Sula airport, encountering the genial, bright-eyed staff, I had to pinch myself. Was this really airport security? This closing charm offensive not only endeared me to this country, but made me instinctively reflect that they truly deserved the great World Heritage Site of Copán.

Sight

13

Seeing beyond Sparta: Mistra

Figure 13 Mistra: The Peribleptos.

'The beauty of Greece lies mainly in contrast, the contrast between stark promontories and blue sea-gulfs and between barren mountain-sides and fertile valleys. Nowhere is the contrast more marked than in the vale of Sparta, Lacedaemon, the "hollow land" of the Homeric age.'
> (Steven Runciman, *Mistra. Byzantine capital of the Peloponnese*,
> London, Thames & Hudson, 1980, 9)

So begins Steven Runciman's elegy for Mistra, the Byzantine capital of the Peloponnese. Mistra, the most exquisitely beautiful of places is an unforgettable combination of peerless art and important Medieval architecture in a place that induces Runciman, the most romantic of modern historians, to rhapsody.

On Easter Sunday, as spring comes to the abandoned town, Mistra is ravishingly beautiful. Located on a sharp pyramidal hill, a wedge standing out from the snow-capped Taygetus mountains, five miles west of Sparta, the ruins are drenched in wild flowers. Here, overlooking the vale of Sparta history is resplendent too. After all Helen was queen of this realm before fleeing Menelaus's palace for Troy. Yet her story, for all its timeless simplicity and much as it might seem preposterous to contemplate, is dwarfed by the expected glories of this lost hilltown where Byzantium made its last abortive stand.

Mistra was a great capital for little more than the blink of an eye in terms of great civilizations. At its zenith, it had 20,000 inhabitants with populous tumbling hillside suburbs beyond its walls. It began, though, as no more than a formidable castle, a serendipitous outcome of the infamous fourth crusade of 1204 when a combination of dissolute Franks and Venetians captured Constantinople, ousted the Byzantine Emperor and wantonly divided up the territorial spoils. The Peloponnese with its heartland at Sparta was won by the self-regarding Villehardouins from Burgundy. Here, in the footsteps of Menelaus, close to ancient Sparta, they made a home at a palace known as La Crémonie. Forty turbulent years passed before William of Villehardouin, scion of the third generation, born in these parts, felt compelled to defend his slice of paradise from the untamed hill tribes in the towering Taygetus mountains. Choosing an uninhabited conical hill known as Myzithra, by 1249 he had erected a great castle that soared intimidatingly above the pastoral valley below. The upstart Villehardouins lasted only a mere dozen years more before the ousted Emperor, Michael Palaeologus reasserted Byzantine supremacy and effectively ended the Latin adventure in Greece. At first, the Emperor, known as a despot, was most interested in the palace in the Spartan vale, but his liberated Greek citizens without fanfare migrated to the steep hill slope below the fortress of Mistra. Water was plentiful and the place was airier than the plain. The orthodox bishop soon joined them and within two decades a new city had discretely taken shape. Keeping track of what happened next in this idyllic spot is unnecessary as emperor followed emperor and usurper after usurper preyed on the political direction of Mistra. Suffice it to say that by the early fifteenth century it had become the cultural capital of the Greek world.

Thanks to many arranged marriages with Latin princesses, here Byzantium and the Latin West found commonality in the creative arts and philosophy. How Mistra's artists were able to convey such sublime serenity despite the perpetual political turmoil is a mystery. This erudite world famously came to a cataclysmic end on 29 May 1453 when Sultan Mehmet II conquered Constantinople. Seven years to the day later, the Sultan's army arrived in front of Mistra. The despot Demetrius confronted reality quickly, surrendered meekly and the next four centuries of this town followed a different, provincial course. The Ottomans treated Mistra with respect until, in 1824, Greek insurgents challenged the murderous Ibrahim, pasha of the Morea. 'I will not cease till the Morea be a ruin', Ibrahim informed a British Government official, and indeed, after unspeakable atrocities, Mistra was abandoned to archaeology. Today, it is a UNESCO world heritage site inhabited by a few shy nuns and their cats in the mid-slope convent of Pantanassa.

Mistra comprises three distinct parts: the Frankish citadel on the summit of the hill, the walled *kastron* in which the palace of despots is to be found, and the walled town itself, known as the *mesochora*. On Easter Sunday I visited only a small part, relishing the prospect of a return visit to see more. Entering the town from the unpretentious main gate to the lower town, I ambled along the cobbled streets to the Peribleptos, then climbed the winding way up to the convent of Pantanassa, before shimmying along the streets to the palace of the despots, from where I bowled down to the cathedral of St. Demetrios with its associated museum.

With a cloudless sky, the bright sunshine made the carpets of flowers bedazzlingly radiant, one so distracting, that I had to concentrate to make sense of the urban dereliction with its noble houses jostling with shops, peasant dwellings, fountains and much besides.

Tucked in the far lower corner of the town is the monastery of the Peribleptos. The deceptively large church is half concealed in a cave. If Mistra was only this church, it would merit world heritage status. Dedicated in about 1358 to the Virgin in the time of the despot Manuel Cantacuzenus, this is an inestimable treat on a par with Giotto's Assisi or, frankly, the Sistine Chapel. Much of the main church is covered in frescoes, numerous scenes conveying an austere dignity to figures whose soft outlines allow them almost to float. A combination of a powdery and a darker hue of blues figure prominently in illuminating the rich iconographic programmes miraculously surviving on just about every wall. Reigning supreme in the dome, of course, is a luminous Christ as Pantocrator. Feast your eyes on Christ's entry into a crowded Jerusalem and the diaphanously dressed priests and angels in heavenly conclave. A metropolitan artist has brought vivid harmony to the incalculable number of light, slender figures. In dazzling scenes, four or more painters have conjured up the authority of Byzantium in its final age. There is both a solemnity to the philosophy and a graceful expressiveness, idioms that were soon to be hallmarks of the early Renaissance in Italian cities.

There is no press of tourists jostling to enter this great church. For a moment, staring at the majestic paintings you catch yourself wondering how this could be. Count your blessings, take a deep breath and then set your sights on the Pantanassa, and the far beacon of its red-tiled domes. The jumble of roofless houses along the alleyways include the grand Phrangopoulos House. A quintessential minor Medieval noble's house, from its first-floor hall – the triclinium – the picture windows take in the sweep of the vale below. Underneath the vaulted undercroft was for storage and stabling. A grander version of this, the house of Lascaris, occupied the mid-slope below. A verandah beyond the triclinium undoubtedly offered an unparalleled spot for cocktails and seasonal dining.

The cats in the Pantanassa look old and thin. They stare with motionless disinterest as you emerge into the convent. Unlike the sumptuous feast of unkempt flowers and grasses around it, this is an oasis of order. A nun peeks out and, like her cats, shows no interest. Above her dormitory on an elevated terrace stands a three-aisled basilica with its two-storey entrance hall and picture-book belfry. It is a solid gothic church, with discrete ornamental sculptured carvings and a well-tempered use of tiles to lend colour as well as provide protection against earthquakes. The last great architectural achievement of the Byzantines, an inscription records its construction in 1428, its paintings are astonishingly well preserved for a building that has remained in constant use for six centuries. The rich cycle of frescoes are less expressive than those of the Peribleptos, but are nevertheless powerful proclamations of the last days of empire. Rich in detail, there is still a strong use of light colours that give an urgency and expressiveness to scenes like the annunciation of the virgin and, again, the entry into Jerusalem (the walled city perhaps being Mistra itself).

Up higher, passing through the unpropitious Monemvasia gate, lies the Palace of the Despots. It is roped off because, notwithstanding the euro crisis, the crazy authorities are re-building it! These elegant buildings form an L-shape around a courtyard. Dating from the mid-thirteenth century, these are a series of successive halls, the loftiest being four storeys high. Modelled upon the Palace of the Porphyrogennetos in Constantinople, it is a harbinger of the palaces that dominate Italy's renaissance piazzas. As if to compound my dismay, believe it or not, a Mercedes has somehow brought a grandee to see the work-in-progress. If the despots were still alive would they be doing the same, I wonder? An insensitive challenge to European best practice in conservation for the benefit of some oligarch or other with pennies to spend.

I weave my way down the cobbled streets, trying to put this aberrant encounter out of my mind. Close to the lower entrance is the multi-domed cathedral dedicated to St Demetrios, known as the Metropolis. It survived in use until the advent of the infamous Ibrahim Pasha and, like any great town cathedral, is a chronicle in stone and imagery to Mistra's episodic history. The light and airy porticoed courtyard invitingly entices one into the sombre church. Again there is a feast of thirteenth-century paintings, defined by their clear and peaceful narration. In the floor of the nave is a marble slab decorated with the twin-headed eagle of the despots. Its survival after centuries of turmoil is perhaps a miracle secured by the awe invoked by its majestic setting.

Overlooking the courtyard is a dinky museum, illuminated by sultry lighting, with clothing, jewellery found in burials and a lapidary section. Being wholly underwhelming I ambled on, determined to carry with me to my Easter lunch the rhapsodic congregation of painted diaphanous figures, mixed with the radiance of Mistra's flora. Towering over ancient Sparta and its vale, the Medieval imagination is unleashed here in all its glory, conveying the final visual triumph of Byzantium on the eve of the Renaissance.

14

Sights and Sanctuary at Saranda

Figure 14 View from Forty Saints looking south over the Straits of Corfu (courtesy of the Butrint Foundation).

'A rough mole encloses a little cothon or basin sufficient for the use of the small boats which alone frequent the harbour, though it would be both secure and convenient for large vessels, were the commerce of this part of Epirus sufficient to require them, as the bay has good anchorage and is well protected both from south-easterly and north-westerly gales; in the latter direction, by a remarkable cape called Kefalì, which with Cape St. Catherine, or the northern extremity of Corfu, forms the entrance of the channel from the northward; in the opposite direction the harbour is protected by the projecting coasts both of the continent and island. Today, though it blows a gale of wind from the southward, there is no sea in the port.'

(William Martin Leake, *Travels in Northern Greece*,

London, J. Rodwell, 1835, 12)

Today the Forty Saints sits discretely above the crowded bay of Saranda, in southern Albania, overshadowed by telephone aerials. Entering the arcing harbour your eye is drawn to the melée of small boys plunging into the water, little sun-tanned minxes in an otherwise sleepy, almost dreamy, tourist town. Saranda's ancient history when it was *Onchesmos* is barely visible. The little walled Roman port where Cicero took ship for Brindisi after vacationing with his friend Titus Pomponius Atticus lies below a forest of new buildings. Only a section of the later city wall, belonging to the sixth century, and the remains of a late Roman synagogue next to it remind visitors that *Onchesmos* was once a place associated with Aeneas's flight from Troy, taking its name from his aged father, Anchises. According to Dionysius of Halicarnassos there was a great temple here dedicated to Aphrodite, but no trace of it has been found. If it existed, the most likely spot would not be close to the narrow beach but high on the shoulder of the steep hill that forms the backdrop for the great bowl which, until very recently, contained Saranda. My guess – and it is a guess – is that the temple lies beneath the huge monument that gave its name to Saranda from the age of the Crusades until now: the church of the Forty Saints.

To reach the Forty Saints you must ascend the long hill leaving Saranda for Gjirokastra and then follow the labyrinth of ill-made roads through a dishevelled suburb out onto the unkempt rump of the hill. Today, the monument is fenced, but the gate is never closed. Press on to the edge of the hill and then experience one of the most satisfying moments to be had in the Mediterranean. Here is a peerless sight. Below lies Saranda of course, squatting in the bay; to the right, as if in a huge plastic diorama, flow the glittering Straits of Corfu, with the upper half of Corfu being crystal sharp to the eye. 'Corfu lies like a sickle beside the flanks of the mainland', Lawrence Durrell reminds us in *The Greek Islands*, 'forming a great calm bay, which narrows at both ends so that the tides are squeezed and calmed as they pass it'. To the left of this celebrated island, immediately to your south, at the end of a meandering peninsula, lies Butrint, ancient *Buthrotum*, tucked behind Lake Butrint. Inland, occupying the foreground before the steep wall of mountains, is a long saddle-backed hill, the Phoinike – according to Polybius, the richest town in this region in Hellenistic times. The sublime pleasure of this breathtaking view is enhanced by the gentle breeze carrying the sea-blown aromas of this hillside, a heady blend of thyme, jasmine and broom.

The view distracts from the sprawling ruins of the Forty Saints that would once have been a gigantic seamark for sailors passing westwards to Sicily or southwards to Greece. No precise connection has yet been discovered that demonstrates the ruined basilica was, in fact, dedicated to the Forty Saints. Indeed, a local tradition tells how only 30 of these were actually saintly; the remaining ten were demons. The 30 true saints are said to have left Saranda, leaving only the ten demons behind.

The Forty Martyrs (later beatified as saints) were themselves soldiers in the army of Licinius who in AD 320 refused to abandon their Christian faith and were made to stand in a frozen pond until they expired. Their cult was widespread in the eastern Mediterranean, and relics are known to have been held at Constantinople and Caesarea. They enjoyed particular veneration in the age of Justinian, and his chronicler, Procopius, records how the Byzantine emperor was cured of a serious infection of the knee when his leg was brought into contact with their relics, which had recently been found in the city.

In late antiquity, judging from the scale of the remains, Santa Quaranta must have been a holy place of some significance in the late Roman world – the architectural vision, we might assume, of an accomplished Holy Man. Luigi Maria Ugolini (the Italian fascist excavator associated with Butrint) who studied the building in the mid-1920s, refers to it as probably the finest of all the churches which he had seen during his travels in Albania. It is certainly the largest basilica of its kind in the region, ranking alongside the episcopal churches at Nikopolis, 100 kilometres to the south in Greece.

The basilica was conceived as a major pilgrimage centre, to attract the faithful from the length of the Adriatic as well as the Balkan interior. Founded shortly before *c.* AD 500, it was served by a monastery that existed until the fourteenth or fifteenth century when it fell victim to the Ottoman conquest of this region. The monastic buildings and hostels for the reception of pilgrims and other guests fell into decay, only to get a new lease of life in the eighteenth and nineteenth centuries during a heady revival of Orthodoxy in Epirus. Then misfortune struck. Santa Quaranta became a redoubt for Greek patriots from the Ionian islands in 1878 who were mercilessly eliminated by Ibrahim Pasha and 6,000 Albanian irregulars. A postcard from the First World War attests to its miserable condition. Nevertheless, its roofless buildings still attracted pilgrims on its saints' day, 9 March; a small community of monks possibly found shelter here. In 1944, so the locals believe, it was a victim of Allied aerial bombing ahead of Operation Houndforce, when 2,000 British marines landed nearby to capture Saranda. Is this apocryphal, I wonder? I suspect its fate was more likely sealed when the communists dynamited it in the 1950s and the shrine atop a peerless Adriatic Sea eerie was transformed into a military camp. On my first visit in 1993, soldiers nervously warned me away. Four years later the camp was abandoned, and so commenced my fascination with this great church.

We made a new survey of the ruins, demonstrating that the church was 43 metres long and 23 metres wide, with a projecting eastern apse. As the Danish architectural historian, Einar Dyggve, showed in 1938, the interior was truly remarkable: a heptaconch, with three large contiguous exedras or conchs on either side, which were of somewhat greater dimensions than the eastern apse. These conchs are contained within the massive lateral walls of the building; the walls of the conchs as well as its eastern apse were apparently pierced by many doors, windows and articulated by niches. Strange as this architectural rhetoric might be, the most intriguing exterior features are the votive inscriptions in red tile, set into the outside walls of the basilica, recording the names and devotion of benefactors who contributed to the cost of erecting it.

Even more remarkable is what lies hidden below this building. Encased within the great raised structure is an extensive and extraordinarily elaborate crypt, a labyrinth of chambers, vaulted halls, passages and chapels underlying the narthex, the south-western flank and the whole western bay of the church. Here tortoises as well as giant spiders find sanctuary. The principal access to this crypt seems to have been from outside the church on the north side, by way of two entrances, the first via a narrow arched opening leading into an impressive series of high-vaulted unlit chambers running across the western end of the church, beneath the narthex, and the second via an opening through the north wall of the church, leading into an annular corridor which runs the whole width of the building. A third entrance may have existed below the southern end of the narthex – leading into a lower-level vaulted space, the heart of the underground complex.

Our survey dated the monastery to the sixth century on the basis of fragments of late fifth- or early sixth-century amphorae used in one of the tile inscriptions on the western façade of the church. Furthermore, roof-tiles, shallow *imbrices*, marked with two finger-swipes width-wise across their wider ends, found on the site around the basilica, are of the same type and fabric as tiles dated to the fifth century at Butrint, 20 kilometres to the south. Justinian surely knew of this mariner's cathedral.

The grand basilica is associated with a modest gaggle of rooms and buildings jammed in the area immediately to its north. A small bath-house, for instance, perhaps for ritual cleansing, stands in front of an entrance into the underground complex. Perhaps the most suggestive discovery is a paved, shallow, oval pond placed beside the apse: is this a miniature replica of the lake where the martyrs froze to death?

In a later, second phase, an imposing outer narthex was constructed against the old western façade of the basilica and the four large vaulted chambers beneath the inner narthex were converted into a large cistern. At this time it appears that the walls of the subterranean chambers were re-plastered and re-painted with a new scheme of decoration. Two dramatic scenes survive in recently discovered patches: the first showing an episode in which Christ seizes the beard of a saintly figure, the second depicting a large boat with a mast and sail, possibly Christ stilling the storm on the Sea of Galilee. The striking painting and the pigments used belong to the ninth or tenth century, when pioneering pilgrims bound for the Holy Land from Adriatic ports in Italy passed below this seamark.

Pilgrims still come here: tell-tale soot-blackened niches below which candle wax has dripped bear witness to the discrete modern faithful who continue to recognize the martyrs on 9 March. Communism failed to eliminate their faith, though Enver Hoxha, Albania's post-war dictator, persecuted priests. No signs, though, inform the visitor of the erstwhile glory of this church and its crypts, let alone its enigmatic metropolitan rhetoric. Commanding such sights this place surely signified the gateway to the Adriatic Sea and the passage to Sicily, a seamark that cannot have failed to command interest even in Constantinople. Today, these undignified ruins superficially resemble those of the illegal houses, recently dynamited by the authorities then left collapsed to puzzle the visitor. Santa Quaranta is badly in need of care worthy of its status.

Later, at Landi's welcoming restaurant by the water's edge, over a plate of red mullet graced by an Epirote white wine, the singular significance of Santa

Quaranta holds me in thrall. It is hard not to draw a connection between the forest of post-communist tourist hotels now filling the confines of this bay and the pilgrimage that made *Onchesmos* a celebrated sanctuary in earlier centuries, and caused the name of the town itself to be altered and become elided into the name of the port – modern Saranda is but a version of Forty Saints.

15

Cavernous Spectacles of Colour: S. Michele at Olevano and the Crypt of the Original Sin

Figure 15 The Virgin Mary in one apse of the Crypt of the Original Sin (courtesy Marco Limoncelli).

The autostrada sweeps east of Vesuvius and leads south past Salerno. Beyond, as Carlo Levi famously observed in his *Christ stopped at Eboli*, this other Italy is poorer, mostly forgotten, mountainous and blissfully rich in archaeology. But it was not always this way. The Bay of Naples, of course, was the centre of the world in late Republican and early Imperial times. It's not surprising, then, that this tract of southern Italy enjoyed an affluent revival once Lombard chiefs took Benevento in the sixth century. Two remarkable places from this Beneventan principality are, believe it or not, improbably located in caves. Each cave exhibits the internationalism and grandiosity of this era, revealing a visual world that is so very different from the depressed state that since early modern times continues to characterize Levi's adopted lands.

Up from the anonymous modern town of Eboli are three hamlets that comprise Olevano sul Tusciano. Contact the commune first and they'll meet you in the compact square of Ariano and likely as not the *protezione civile* team will take you in a jeep from the nineteenth-century hydro-electric plant up the twisting steep white track that leads up the mountainside to the sanctuary of S. Michele. It is eight kilometres before you have to climb by foot for a further kilometre through thick woodland. As you struggle up, bear in mind thousands from Olevano do it every Michaelmas, the saint's day, the truly heroic serving as porters of a seventeenth-century statue that otherwise resides in the cave-sanctuary itself. The closed twelfth-century front of the overhanging cave mouth conceals an extraordinary grandiosity. Pause to take in the vertiginous panorama reaching towards Salerno Bay, a stone's throw from Paestum. Time and again, you'll ask, why here?

Even as the door in the closure wall opens, it is not quite clear as to what lies ahead. Excavations to the left and right by Alessandro di Muro of Cosenza University show that there was a seventh-century building in the cave mouth, overlain by first an eighth–ninth-century hostel for pilgrims, then a larger tenth–eleventh-century version. To the right lay a ninth-century baptistery, associated with which Alessandro found fifteen ceramic acquamaniles, pots with the strangest ornamentation, reminiscent of Abbasid or even Chinese figures of the age.

Ahead lie modern stairs, drawing one up steeply into the cave. Beyond in the immediate half-light are two of the seven churches, dwarfed by the cathedral-like chasm. The smaller domed church (B) is virtually complete, with exquisitely stuccoed windows. Turn-of-the-millennium paintings grace its exterior too, but these are mere appetizers for the glorious church (A) to its right. The seventeenth-century statue of S. Michele sits before the altar, surrounded by an almost complete cycle of vivid paintings dating to the turn of the millennium. This is Olevano's modern sanctuary church, a precious age-old shrine to a combination of saints as the cave's purpose was annexed by an ambitious bishop of Salerno.

A steep, original, winding stairway lures one deeper into the cave past two other shrines. We inched onwards and up and then, before the ground tumbled away into the darkness, we shuffled into the small domed church (G). Bang up against the wall Alessandro shone his torch and beckoned me to peer closely. Carved into the Dark Age plaster were thousands of graffiti, momentoes of pilgrims from everywhere. With supreme pleasure he pointed out Roffrid, almost certainly an Anglo-Saxon. As yet unstudied, these walls contain an extraordinary registry of visitorship to this dank, dark place. But the pilgrimage did not end here. Into the chasm charged Alessandro, our steps discomforting the bevy of bats that inhabit the overhang at this point. Descending into a craggy niche, we arrived at a basin beside a carved pillar of rock where, it seems, the ultimate sacred ablutions occurred. There was not even a half-light here, so in the early Middle Ages this was surely purgatory after which release back into the lighted mouth of the cave was redemption.

The sublime pleasure of this place is its rawness measured by the skilful analysis that Alessandro has brought to bear to interpret its half-lit art, architecture and archaeology. I want to say that nothing quite compares to it. But, then there is the so-called Sistine Chapel of the South.

Past Eboli, head for Potenza, and a miserable road through wild landscapes leads on to Matera, the World Heritage City with a museum given over to Carlo Levi's neo-realistic paintings. Matera has cave churches, in amongst the *sassi*, the hundreds of rock-cut houses. Flocks of kestrels swarm like swifts over these, their insistent mewing being the sound-track to full immersion into Medieval living. But Matera's most wondrous asset lies seven kilometres outside the city.

To see the Crypt of the Original Sin, you must book online (www.criptadelpeccatooriginale.it), then drive to a service station on the Potenza road. A group of us have booked for 11am and, like magic, a young man arrives in a minibus, checks us off on his clipboard and chatters away. This is no member of the state Soprintendenza: he is part of a cooperative, and from the outset emits service culture 101 with a genuine smile. We follow, a crocodile line of seven or eight vehicles, taking an unmarked side-road through a new vineyard, passing the winery itself, before we halt above a craggy canyon running like a gash through this stark Basilicata landscape. A path takes us down to the 'Crypt'; inside, in the pitch black, we are invited by our guide to sit on the inclined rock floor. Once settled, he throws a switch, the light brings to life a solitary painted fresco; with this our guide delivers his dramatic presentation.

Honestly, I expected to hate it. Instead, like my companions in the gloom, I was captivated. With a certain theatricality, first the three apses on the rocky east wall were illuminated, followed by the incomparable inner, south wall. My eyes were drawn instantly to the starkly naked bodies of Adam and Eve. Discovered only in the 1960s and recently conserved, this is an unexpected visual feast.

The three apses are beautifully painted with an array of saints, of whom St. Peter – representing the influence of Rome – is the most prominent. The Madonna with child in her arms, serenely graces the middle apse. Any church would be proud of such majestic figural painting. But the testimony to creation on the east wall trumps anything I've seen from this era. At one end, light and darkness are featured as full figures standing above a liturgical scene depicting the washing of hands with an acquamanile of the type found only at Olevano. A sumptuous palm draws the eye, separating these scenes from an imposing numb-eyed creator and his voluptuous creations, within which is a second tree around which a menacing serpent has wound itself. Poppies fill the white plastered field occupied by these busy people, emitting a spectacle of brilliant colour. Once accustomed to the light, as though this was a Palaeolithic cave, one's eyes are drawn to minor fragments of painting like the shield of the armed soldier to the left of the apses. How mesmerizing this place must have been in the half-light emitted from the diminutive glass lamps of the age.

All I can say is this place is as sublimely dazzling as the Sistine Chapel, and, paradoxically, a lot more comfortable to visit. Of course, this is not a crypt, and it has nothing to do with Byzantium, as much of the local literature suggests. Painters from Beneventan transformed this small mid ninth-century church, possibly for funerary purposes, providing it with indisputable iconographic echoes of painting in Rome. Nevertheless, in visual conception, with imagery that leaps from codices of the time, it was clearly the work of someone living on the frontier with a resurgent Byzantium keen to demonstrate his ideological loyalties. Here, we might imagine, those pilgrims who inscribed their names at Olevano, paused in yet another riff on purgatory before traipsing southwards towards the Byzantine port of Otranto, where they then took a ship to the Holy Land.

After such an unexpectedly glorious experience, managed with supreme skill by our service-conscious guide, dinner was obligatory. Matera does not disappoint. Challenged by the stigma of Carlo Levi's tract, it boasts restaurants worthy of the Crypt of the Original Sin. I sinned with a fragrant local Basilicata moscato, Terre di Orazio, to accompany peerless appetizers and a *maialino* to die for. Frankly, as will be obvious, I am not cut out to be a pilgrim, but I can understand from the visual riches dating from the early Medieval Principality of Benevento why one might consider it.

16

A Renaissance Dream House at Visegrád

Figure 16 Visegrád: a view of the reconstructed Renaissance palace on the Danube.

Forty minutes north of Budapest, on a bend in the Danube, occupying a strategic point on its western side, lies Visegrád. In Roman times, this was a heavily fortified stretch of the Pannonian *limes*, controlling some of the richest farming land in Europe. Today, though, its real fascination lies in how Hungary's smallest town became a Hungarian royal stronghold and then, since the 1930s, a symbol of Hungary's Medieval and Renaissance monumentality in the heart of Europe. On a magical autumnal day in November, I had the good fortune to visit Visegrád with Professor József Laszlovszky and his new cohort of Masters' students (in Medieval Studies) from the Central European University in Budapest.

Visegrád lies in the shadow of Budapest in most respects. Their relationship to the Danube as a great axiomatic line both connecting and separating Europe underscores about every episode in their common histories up until our times, the age of cultural tourism. So, as I shall explain, the great castle of Buda that dominates Hungary's capital is a textbook example of artful restoration and a benchmark for the equally extraordinarily audacious restoration at Visegrád. Largely obliterated in the savage battle for Budapest in December 1944, post-war governments have skilfully re-invented the Medieval character of this Danubian castle. More accurately, establishing a genesis for the Austro-Hungarian city following the steady loss since 1918 of much of Greater Hungary's once far-flung territories has been an important task for generations of the country's dedicated archaeologists and conservators. Not surprisingly, then, the Medieval fortress of Visegrád, rightly celebrated today, draws huge numbers of tourists. Wonder, as you might, gazing down from this formidable eerie on the nineteenth-century city below, as a feat in shaping an historical story, Buda actually pales in comparison to Visegrád. Here – amongst the constellation of monuments – is a thought-provoking early Renaissance Pompeii.

Visegrád was first mentioned in a royal text of 1009. Hungarian kings came to hunt in the rolling hill-country that occupies this corner of the Danube, today a wooded national park criss-crossed by trails. József has thoughtfully contrived the order of our visit. We begin at the top, close to the upper citadel belonging to this small town, from where, in the hard pewter-coloured light, the entire landscape can be viewed. Of course, the listless Danube in its huge setting draws one's eye, but then there is the thirteenth-century upper castle, contrived to belong to a Grand Tourist's lithograph. Its crenellated battlements and turrets, evocatively restored as if for a film, command the river as it narrows through the wooded hills before it turns towards Budapest. Countless romantic images depict it, a place of wild middle-European Medieval royals, on a great fluvial highway connecting the west to the east. The modern restoration, like fortress Buda, naturally draws coachloads to its dark fastness. But its history was marginal in the annals of Visegrád. On a lower ledge, immediately below the citadel, is its precursor, and lower still, out on a point, is the Tower of

Solomon, another romantic viewshed. The precursor on Sibrik Hill between the two textbook castles is no more than a few stone courses high. This unrestored castle was a well-placed fourth-century Roman fortress, parts of which, recent excavations have shown, were maintained until the twelfth century. Being the remains of an imperial interloper, aimed at keeping the menacing Germans and Huns bottled up on the east bank of the Danube in the Migration Period, there has been no attempt to rebuild the camp. But its place in Visegrád's history has not been entirely forgotten. On the millennial anniversary of the first reference to the township, in 2009, with a sketchy allusion to an eleventh-century prisoner held here, the modern followers of the Knights of St. George chose this undistinguished fortress to erect a Disneyesque monument, a broad sword with its blade sunken into a deep stone.

Gazing at this brazen historical statement, as if by magic, military drums strike up in the Tower of Solomon below. Knights are jousting, József tells us with a twinkle in his eye, their enthusiastic and guttural cries travelling crisply across the misty autumnal woodland. Following the path downwards, passing through its upper gatehouse we reach the source of the jousting, a much-restored thirteenth-century tower. With walls five metres wide, this keep occupies the lowest concealed ledge directly below the citadel. Here, brightly attired, melodramatically, the busy knights are being put through their martial paces: capacity building in perfecting their archery, throwing knives, and other everyday Medieval skills. The tower was erected with the overt purpose of enjoying the visual pleasure of this Danubian panorama. Its riverside rooms were graced by high windows, worthy of a late Romanesque cathedral. Not surprisingly, this bastion was the magnet for a series of sieges culminating in 1544 with an Ottoman raid that caused part of it to collapse. That, perhaps, accounts for the most unexpected restoration I have ever encountered. Its Medieval features are capped, so-to-speak, by a remodelling of its uppermost floors made in communist times. To re-purpose the tower for popular effect, concrete has been deployed: onto the Romanesque has been grafted Cold War bunker architecture. Unfortunately, concrete rots, unlike the masterful stonework of the Medieval architect. Twenty years from now this conundrum will pose a baffling and expensive challenge for the Hungarian authorities if Solomon's Tower is to be maintained for modern knights and tourists.

On we go as a group, following the path from the lower gate, through the town clinging to the lower slopes until we arrive at Visegrád's main monument – the Renaissance palace. I was quite unprepared for this benign assault upon my visual senses. Pannonian (Roman) fortresses and feudal castles swarming with burly shaven-headed faux actors did not really surprise me as much as the coachloads of Chinese tourists. By contrast, the palace is a heritage theorist's dream: discovered accidentally in the 1930s below centuries of colluvium that had tumbled from the sharp slope reaching to the upper citadel, this fifteenth-century utopian venture really is a Florentine Pompeii – it's been unearthed and reassembled to serve contemporary aims. Palaces from Florence and similar Tuscan oases seem to have been uppermost in the mind of its Danubian architects. Medieval archaeology is normally never given such grandiose treatment; such expansive reconstruction is reserved for Minoan, Greek or Roman monuments as most nations expediently conclude that if the palace actually survives in Italy, why invest in returning it to its former glory. There was, of course, a reason.

In 1335, the kings of Bohemia, Poland and Hungary met here to define themselves as the Visegrád countries, a precursor of many modern pacts. Released from the entrapment of communism in 1991, the newly elected Prime Minister of Hungary, József Antall, repeated this late-Medieval meeting at Visegrád, inviting Václav Havel of Czechoslovakia and Lech Wałesa of Poland to re-affirm a treaty then six centuries old. The re-enactment, marking the closure of the Cold War, was a celebration of verbal diplomacy rather than martial exhibitionism. Since then, these V4 countries (with the division of Czechoslovakia) have met regularly as a group, tracing their collective roots to this Medieval town and its dream house. The connection brought satisfying resources to Hungary's archaeologists as well as a modern purpose.

First conceived by King Charles I around 1325, the palace was enlarged in two bold steps by King Louis I and King Sigismund. The next chapter here belongs to a king elected from outside the royal lineage: Matthias Corvinus (1443–1490). Insecurity about his birth may explain much about the zenith of the palace at Visegrád. Its specific inspiration, though, surely resulted from the young monarch's marriage to an Italian beauty, Beatrice, daughter of the King of Naples. One issue of this amorous union was an audacious re-fashioning of the earlier buildings into a majestic, square complex constructed around a colonnaded courtyard with suites of rooms worthy of the Arno valley. Now, almost everything has been re-built with great attention to archaeological detail. For purists it is a nightmare, dwarfing Sir Arthur Evans's reconstruction of the Minoan palace at Knossos. Yet in this case, of course, there were written descriptions, some sketches and plenty of parallels. Far from being vulgar, every effort has been made to retain the original colour scheme, and to furnish each room with the assistance of contemporary paintings. Perhaps the most remarkable discoveries were the red 'marble' fountains. Dominating the quad of the main palace is a full-size marble replica of the Hercules fountain, the remains of which (now restored from thousands of fragments) exist in the two-room museum. Made by a master imported from Italy (of course), this breathtaking work of art must have astonished central European visitors to the Hungarian court.

The museum also includes an original Regensburg stove, a colossal corner oven completely covered in lustrous lead-green tiles, each bearing the coats of arms of properties of the illustrious owner. This vaunting audacity did not end in the main building. Matthias's legacy was to overhaul everything. The philosopher-king, much enthused with the ideas of Plato's Republic, also rebuilt the kitchen, private quarters, grand church and gardens (with imported pleasure plants), to the extent that soon you as a simple visitor are visually seduced, as presumably his Neapolitan queen was, to feel as though this could be central Italy – but nine-tenths is truly fake and modern.

Managed as an outpost by the National Museum in Budapest, this is Medieval archaeology on a bold scale. Eighty years of intermittent research excavations, restoration and thoughtful display mean that this is no Las Vegas. The range of ceramics, glasses and household knick-knacks in the museum have all the more meaning because you've walked through the rooms from which these have come.

Two final points about Visegrád. First, the National Museum has made the ultimate children's playground in front of the palace – a place of gaily painted wooden swings and ships and see-saws. Needless to say, 'King Matthias' greets the children on entering and offers entrancing rustic pleasures rather than a commonplace plastic one. Second, for the palate, there's the Renaissance restaurant. With waiters dressed for the age of Da Vinci and with tableware worthy of the neighbouring royal households, the food while allegedly Medieval, is first class, as are the beverages. Budapest, then, is undoubtedly glorious; Visegrád is an unexpected treat, an assault on the senses as benign and memorable as that first view of the great river that gave visual reason to its special history.

Smell

17

The Smell of the Desert: Doha and Al Zubarah

Figure 17 Doha's Museum of Islamic Art and the Gulf junks that moor in its shadow.

Doha's Hamad international airport is conceived as a colossal Bedouin tent. Its unvarnished immensity along with the neatly robed and polite customs agents tells all: at a stroke, the idea of the World Cup being held here makes perfect sense. Building and managing the stadia in 2022 is no issue. In the footsteps of age-old planners and architects from Hippodamos of Miletus onwards, the Qatari will efficiently bring it off. After two days here I began to wonder if they might control the weather too. Qatar has to be seen to be believed.

I was in Doha to lecture at UCL Qatar, partner of Hamad Bin Khalifa University in Education City. Like everything else, this has been envisioned by the Qatar Foundation on a gigantic scale to provide five-star education to young Qataris, principally women, and for other international students. José

Carvajal Lopez, Lecturer in Islamic Archaeology, introduced me to the library, conservation and material labs, each of which lives up to this new nation's vaunting expectations. Top notch in every way, UCL Qatar, for its part, is training a generation to ensure that the present Qatari vision endures in its civic society long past the exhaustion of oil and gas reserves.

Scale is everything in this new metropolis of 2 million, effectively created since the 1960s for 200,000+ Qataris, most of whom had been pearl fishers until that time. Fifty years ago, Doha was a small gulf town. Today, frenzied highways of Los Angeles proportions connect the airport by way of the Corniche to West Bay, Katara, and, of course, quarters like Education City. West Bay, built mostly on landfill, has been constructed since about 2006, and dwarfs mid-town Manhattan. The architectural rhetoric of the forest of illuminated and mostly marbled skyscrapers at West Bay pays homage to global business and its paladins. But Islamization is important to Qatar, and at the vast new restaurant and shopping districts of Katara and the Souq Waqif, swish pastiches of Arab architecture, make Edward Said's 'Other' palatable and even seductive to all-comers. In defence of this self-conscious Islamization, evident pleasure was being had by young Qatari families everywhere I looked. The atmosphere is Mediterranean, inclusive and most definitely inviting.

The paradox of this metropolitan vision is that Qatar has a very modest urban history. Apart from Doha, which grew up as a small Gulf port, the only other settlement of any size was Al Zubarah, inscribed in 2013 as Qatar's first UNESCO World Heritage Site. Situated on the peninsula's north-west coast, directly opposite Bahrain, it seems a million miles from the pulsating metropolis of Doha. This metaphorical distance, amounting to about 80 kilometres, is accentuated by nearly 70 kilometres of absolutely emptied limestone desert. Largely featureless and unforgiving, save for the occasional small flock of sheep, these are the lands that the Qataris aim to transform into a verdant Garden of Eden with desalinized water.

Visible from at least 10 kilometres away, the 1930s fort of Zubarah proudly commands the far rim of this arid landscape, signalling an oasis of sorts. Built close to the port of the same name, it guarded a well of sweet water, next to the inlet around which the eighteenth-century town was created. Is the fort another pastiche from the age of Hollywood legionnaires? Not at all, made of mud-brick with near perfect crenellations, it houses an excellent exhibit introducing Al Zubarah. The UNESCO World Heritage Site itself – 'the ruins' – lie a kilometre away across the flats, reached by way of a beaten track. Three site panels in front of the old city fortifications spell out the importance of this lost town.

Al Zubarah was first settled in the 1760s, a beach-side emporium of tents and huts used seasonally by craftsmen and traders who provided an interface between the Gulf Sea merchantmen and the desert nomads. Mohammed bin Khalifa changed this, erecting fortifications in 1768. A trading town of 6,000 people with at least one palace quickly took shape. In 1799 it was sacked by Omanis, an unpleasant harbinger of the comprehensive destruction of the town by the Sultan of Muscat in 1811. Left in ruins, it reverted to a community of huts and tents. A subsequent generation reinvented Al Zubarah as a pearl fishing community. Within a reduced walled area, about 1,500 fishermen enjoyed new prosperity, and even withstood shelling by a British gunboat in 1874. Four years later, it was once again ensnarled within a spate of regional dissension, and this time left to the sand and wind. Its pearl fishermen moved to Bahrain, then a British Imperial protectorate.

What town, you'll be tempted to ask? Then, passing through the low fortifications with their drum towers, all becomes clear. Before you as far as the eye can see lies a sandy sea of lumps and bumps, a desert version of an English deserted Medieval village on a gigantic scale. Since 2009, a team from Copenhagen University, collaborating with the Qataris, forming the Qatar Islamic Archaeological Heritage Project, has opened up sizeable areas, mere pinpricks given the sprawling scale of the place. This is the latest mission that began with the 1956–1964 Danish Gulf Expedition, and was briefly followed by a survey in 1973 directed by the indefatigable Beatrice de Cardi. A palace complex with an internal courtyard and the largely backfilled remains of the souk are two obvious points to visit. The palace has been cleverly conserved to resist the ever-present menace of shifting sand. At each site the modest efficacy of the mud-brick architecture is apparent. Like the later fort, there is a profound absence of rhetoric about these buildings, designed to inhabit a normally ferocious climate. Judging by the finds from these excavations, the community lived in material splendour with porcelains from China and a rich array of Ottoman consumer goods including tell-tale coffee cups and clay pipes.

The wind-cemented sand, glistening with salt, cracks like ice as you cross it. The air is clean, smelling of the desert, of sun-baked rock. Sustaining this monument will prove some feat, though given its importance to Qatar, its future is secure. I don't doubt the desert here will be tamed. Running along the shoreline, though, is a black vein of oil that washed up after the first Gulf War in 1990, a reminder of the continuing issues that form the spine of Al Zubarah's narrative as a place. More pleasing, though, are the occupants of this marine interface that have outlived the episodes of aggression and abandonment: oyster catchers and sandpipers, command the seashore. Momentarily, on this fresh January day this could be Burnham Sands in Norfolk.

Doha began life as a smaller version of Al Zubarah. Fragments of buildings from the 1930s have survived the frenzy of construction. Rob Carter with UCL Qatar students has made a valiant effort to record these before gigantic towers swallow them up. Together, we examined a wall here and a surviving section of stratigraphy there, but old Doha is no more.

Out beyond the Corniche from where the port once lay, hundreds of dhows sit at anchor; today these are pleasure crafts. Here, too, occupying an artificial point, is I.M. Pei's majestic Museum of Islamic Art. In its isolation, with a narrow driveway bisected by a Tivoli-like cascade, this building is in an altogether different class. If there is pastiche, it is to harbour a germ of its origin in the Alhambra at Granada. Like the Alhambra, Pei's building is both a palace and a fortress and plays with the senses using light and water in a deeply affecting combination. Inside, however, the museology is comfortingly traditional. Long galleries in a darkness illuminated by pin-prick fibre optics house the jewels of Islamic art. Peerless ceramics and treasures – trophies of the Umayyads and Abbasids, and even the early Ottomans – are committed to glass cases that could be in the Metropolitan Museum in New York. 'The Other' of Islam is given no special voice, unlike the tidy little exhibit at Al Zubarah fort. Take a close look at an Ottoman map of the Mediterranean from the sixteenth century, and appreciate that the world could be readily turned upside down and viewed not from the Renaissance or Venice, but by mapmakers with connections to Edo and China. The map, though, is treated as a wall hanging.

This museum speaks volumes about the ongoing transformation of Islam and Qatar, in particular, as it comes to terms with its own history as opposed to the western prism through which it has been viewed. With time, no doubt, the exhibitions will be revamped with more confidence, to connect the world of Qatar today to the extraordinary art of the Islamic past. How am I so sure? Well, the coffee area in the atrium, beyond a gushing fountain, with its brazen view of West Bay, heralds a new standard. This is a twenty-first-century answer to the floating tea-house at Istanbul's Topkapi Palace or the restaurant at the Met overlooking Central Park and Midtown's towers. Here is a vision that summons up a new nation with an eye on the world that was and the world that cloud-based technologies coupled with resources now make realizable.

18

Smelling Spices in Sana'a

Figure 18 Rada': the Medieval town where Roberto Nardi restored the Amiriya Madrasa, 2005 (courtesy Roberto Nardi).

Khaled in Tullo was the first person to mention 11 September 2001 to me. Visitors to his hilltop town numbered in the hundreds every day before the infamous attack; now, he lamented, there was only the occasional tourist. Yemen has sadly become associated with terrorism and tribal wars, yet the reality, notwithstanding its ubiquitous poverty, is a country of bubbly, friendly people.

I came to attend a seminar organized by Roberto Nardi on the occasion of the opening of the newly restored prayer hall of the Amiriya Madrasa at Rada', three hours' drive south of Yemen's capital, Sana'a. Nardi's team had been commissioned by an international consortium to undertake the painstaking restoration of the glorious frescoes and stuccos which once graced the hall. For nearly three years, working on 45-day rotas, a team of a dozen or so Italians lived in near-isolation in a mud-brick house in a back-street of Rada', making the five-minute walk to the ostentatious Amiriya Madrasa alongside the well-preserved Medieval castle.

From my days spent on the Euphrates at Zeugma I was already familiar with the dedication of Nardi's team from the Centro di Conservazione di Roma (CCA), but the conditions at Rada' were altogether startling.

The three-hour drive from Sana'a to Rada' traverses a high mountain pass. The sunlight is intense, but, given the altitude at well-over 2,000 metres, the air is bone dry. The landscape is vast, with Disneyesque hilltop towns occupying rocky outcrops surrounded by oceans of abandoned semi-desert. Close to, the towns are gathered around tall castles. The houses themselves are mostly made of mud-brick, and invariably, if old, elegantly ornamented. The journey is punctuated by armed road-blocks, as often as not connoting the border between one mountain sheikdom and another. All journeys require visas, so our courier passes out seemingly infinite photocopies of our official permission to pass to Rada'.

Rada' itself was once a great late Medieval centre with a sprawling castle of Caernarvon proportions at its heart. Now, though, much of it is derelict, with shattered houses surviving alongside others elegantly curated by attentive owners. Beside the castle stands the Amiriya Madrasa – a huge palatial concept dating to 1504, when thanks to the profits of Indian Ocean trade taken at Aden, the Sultan Amr bin Abd al Wahab (1489–1517) was able to finance numerous great enterprises. This project for a prayer school included a glorious shrine on its first floor, where the luminescent paintings and rococo stuccos remained in a tolerable state until modern times. Since 1982 there had been plans to restore these late Renaissance age works to their original brilliance. Nardi and his team have done just this. The result is simply astonishing. Entering through an atrium, its mud-brick surface burnished and now painted a glistening white, one encounters a whirl of colours that, like a kaleidoscope, leave one breathlessly tracing images and ideas in the extraordinary artistic geometry. Nothing, absolutely nothing, could contrast more strikingly with the blighted decay of the surrounding streets where the souk, in almost every sense, brings to life the kind of townscapes I associate with the desultory and baffling end of antiquity. Here are elegant townhouses alongside a primitive smithy; a taverna of the most rudimentary kind alongside a walled garden. The urban fabric is rich in archaeological detail. Soon, we were discovered by flocks of barefoot children, resembling sparrows looking for crumbs.

By contrast, Tullo, a high-altitude town, still contained within massive Medieval defences, has benefited from recent tourism. Here, cheerful gangs of children trip gaily along the narrow streets. Once again the architecture conveys the sense of a time when Yemen was wealthy and boasted buildings as grand as Renaissance palaces. This lost age, of course, is best preserved at Sana'a itself where the immense medieval and early modern city is almost entirely preserved as a UNESCO World Heritage Site. As often as not, World Heritage Sites leave me asking why was this place inscribed? What makes the place globally significant? What sets it apart? Not Sana'a. An imperious architectural confection, it brings to mind Manhattan. Seemingly thousands of towering mud-brick buildings, as often as not with their apertures picked out by bright paint, conjure up an eclectic mixture of western experiences – early classical, art deco, post-modernism, etc. Yet the effect, transformed by the bubbling existence of a massive souk in the very heart of the old town, like the paintings in the prayer-hall at Rada', transcends all expectations. Best of all is the half-covered market of spices, a patchwork quilt of colours infused with conflicted scents that leave you reeling. Vermilions, russets, sables, even an off-purple, making a paint box spectrum. In no special order, hanging from the eaves, are tightly woven festoons of more plants and roots. Who could conceivably want so much spice? Close your eyes, listen to the awkward nasal cries of the hawkers, then inhale the wafting odours of the treats they are vending. Is this the perfume of paradise?

Yemen, of course, is not without its grave problems. The most startling, without doubt, is the almost ubiquitous consumption of the mild narcotic, qat. Come two o'clock just about every man – and now a growing number of women – begin chewing what appears to be a kind of grass. Very soon, with the unconscious mastication in the mouth, one or other of the cheeks balloons up to appear as if the individual has mumps. On and on they chew all afternoon, resembling goats as their dazed eyes lose any light, until by early evening, almost in unison, the men spit the leaves out, when in cafes into strategically located cans. Drivers, soldiers, policemen, farmers, coffee-drinkers, barmen, shopkeepers, bellboys – everyone chews. The narcotic is probably harmless enough, but the problem lies in the volume of water it takes to cultivate the qat. According to a visiting UN official, the World Bank has told the president that Yemen will exhaust its water resources before long if its men continue to consume qat in such quantities. Given its cultural importance, the palpable poverty and the compelling need to keep the previously well-armed fractious tribes of Yemen calm, the government is in a quandary.

Notwithstanding such issues, Yemen is a remarkable country. Two images are indelible. Its children convey a sense of impish fun, brimming with playfulness and are totally uninhibited. As such, it seems like a young country. More to the point, it is a welcoming country. As I left Sana'a airport, on a midnight flight, the customs officer asked me where I came from. Expecting the worst, I replied a little curtly. He did not notice. 'Did you like Yemen?' he enquired. 'Yes', I said cheerily. 'Then please do think of returning.' 'I certainly will', I confidently replied as he graciously waved me towards my plane.

19

The Disturbing Scent of Gold: Roşia Montană, Transylvania

Figure 19 Relief on our faces: surviving the Roman mines at Roşia Montană – the late Willem Willems (left), David Miles and the author (right), 2014.

There were no vampires to be seen as Wizz flew us low over Transylvania, aiming for Cluj. Forests and rolling open hills were more reminiscent of French pastoral serenity, than the capital of Vlad the Impaler or the devlish Pied Piper. Cluj is the capital of Transylvania, in all but name following its secession to Romania in 1918, and has regained its Roman name – Cluj Napoca. Part of Roman Dacia, created by Trajan in pursuit of gold and other precious minerals, it is my point of departure for a gold mine at Roşia Montană and an encounter with its mining archaeologists.

Roşia Montană lies two hours away in the heart of the undulating Apuseni massif. A mining community since Saxon miners in the fourteenth century rediscovered Roman adits, it prospered under the Habsburgs and continued to be exploited under the communists in the post-war era. But with democracy, following the grisly end of the Ceauşescus in 1989, the galleries were closed and the miners joined the droves of Transylvanians who quit these hills and joined a disenchanted diaspora in Bucharest or further afield in Italy. On the brink of complete extinction, a lifeline was thrown to the community by a Canadian mining company who fancied their chances of panning more gold from these hills using hi-tech methods. Before starting operations they followed Romanian (and international) prescriptions for meeting cultural heritage and environmental standards. I was invited to see how competently the company had met its cultural heritage obligations because, after 17 years of plugging away, they are on the brink of throwing in the towel, frustrated by a miasma of opponents. For the people of Roşia Montană this would be a tragedy; for those who love Roman archaeology, it is a veritable calamity.

Let me explain.

Alba Iulia was the gold-panning capital in Roman times. The Emperor Trajan's army built the town and its Klondike success lasted less than two centuries until the Romans withdrew in AD 271. Inscriptions and wax tablets record at least one mining company operating on behalf of the imperial government, attracting miners from Illyria to Dacia. Prospection covered the forested, hill region, known from tombstones as Alburnus Maior. Serendipitously, Roşia Montană, towards the northern edge of the ancient mining region, has the excavated remains belonging to this pioneering episode that staved off Rome's economic crisis.

Without doubt the most evocative surface remains are to be found at Bucium. Straddling several high wooded hills, with 360 degrees of breathtaking views, this remote place is still occupied by timeless shepherds – hardy, self-reliant men – and their flocks. This is a fossilized, ancient industrial landscape *par excellence*. Everything is Roman in date: two centuries worth of workings, abandoned without any later interventions. Surface adits run for hundreds of yards. Then there are panning pools and, so it is said, deep mines into the uppermost hill. Dotted around too, like low, rabbit pillow mounds, are grassy tumuli, some of which have been recently excavated revealing the modest gifts of ceramic cups and glasses made to the gods by miners' families in memory of loved ones.

By contrast, Roşia Montană is a modern mining landscape with isolated tracts of relic farms, a tradition shaped by almost a millennium. The modern village dates mostly from the nineteenth century, though its roots are probably Medieval. It is the remains of Trajanic Dacian's industrial efforts that have really brought us here. The surface Roman archaeology is provincial in character. Probed at great cost, thanks to the Canadian mining company, parts of the bath-house belonging to the administrative complex have been excavated, as have their temples and parts of their cemeteries including an ashlar-built circular tumulus imitating Augustus's mausoleum in Rome. Diligently published, the surface archaeology reveals the presence of different Roman communities, their investment in worship and the afterlife. All attests to a modest prosperity. Much the same might be said of the present village dating from the heyday of the Habsburg mines, now majestically restored. Notable for its tall-towered churches, tributes to the differing faiths of the miners, and the sizeable miners' houses, Roşia Montană is a showcase historic village. An elegant museum tells the story of the mining township. However, these surface remains are, of course, no more than the tip of the iceberg.

Before going underground, Călin Tămaş from the University of Cluj's geology department, who assisted Beatrice Cauuet of the University of Toulouse, the director of the underground mining research, prepared us for what lay in store. Quite simply, his brilliant exposition led me to two deductions: this is one of the great world-class archaeological projects of recent years, and these mining archaeologists are either insane or simply heroic pioneers.

The next morning, suitably attired in helmet and lamp, thick overalls, and wellingtons, we motored up to the quarried slopes of Mt. Cârnac. After posing outside a boarded up mine entrance, somewhat pensively we followed Călin into the pitch black. The cloying chill is immediate, and our pin-prick lamps illuminate the slushy brown mud underfoot. Passing blocked-up Habsburg tunnels and abandoned modern shafts, we trudged on and on, over mounds of recent fallen tunnel sides, defying the darkened claustrophobia. After an age we arrived at a vertical satanic cavern down which, at several levels, with

70 kilometres of mapped galleries, were tracts of remaining Roman mines. I baulked at the vertigo and decided that only the fearless were made for the nightmarish descent to see short surviving lengths of Roman mining. This place is for Călin, Indiana Jones and similar fit heroes. Being ordinary folk, once out in the sunshine, I was tacitly exultant to have survived, released from the invasive damp and the smell of ores.

Now, Mt. Cărnac, if the mining company proceeds, will be largely obliterated, then reconstituted. Its heroically documented mines will disappear. But let's be rational about this loss. Conserving the mines in the satanic chasms of this hill will cost more than conserving the Colosseum; in addition, these will require an annual upkeep of millions. This is why the mining company has boldly come up with an alternative.

The Cătălina Monulești mine is entered from the village. Duck-walks, railings in places, and lighting have been installed, all the necessary accoutrements for the faint-hearted fans of the Romans. No mud, roof falls, and black holes. No disturbing smell of damp. Inside is a treat, carefully excavated and documented, ready for publication, and made safe for the public. The trail takes an hour, and passes through long lengths of mines supported by posts inserted by ingenious Roman engineers. Down tight, exactly shaped trapezoidal shafts penetrated in the second century, we pass the remains of a vertical wooden water-wheel employed to drain water from the galleries. Up cut steps and through this labyrinth, we reach a kinked branch where Roman miners working on two different alignments cunningly shifted angle to meet up. Lamp niches for the little ceramic spotlights of the age tell their tale. Most of all we see un-emptied Roman galleries: the fallen fill is almost fossilized and must be picked out before shuffling backwards with buckets of debris to dispose of it in unwanted modern galleries. Then there are galleries with recent roof falls; these are unsafe and awaiting a decision as to whether the Canadians will fund their clearance. Logistically this project makes underwater archaeology look like child's play.

The Canadian mining company has spent over $11 million dollars conserving the Cătălina Monulești galleries. Their audacity is simply breathtaking: a peerless museological experience, safe and sustainable has been realized at a cost that governments will not pay. Has the mining company met its obligations, I was asked? Let me put it another way: how many other great European archaeological projects have been published, conserved and then made into museums in recent times? The elemental impact of this research upon Romanian archaeological standards cannot be overstated. As a result, the Canadians, perhaps unwittingly, have entered the annals of archaeology. Possibly their greatest sin is not to know it!

The die-hard opponents of the mine say that renewed gold mining will destroy Roşia Montană's ecology and history. How the truth has been disturbingly twisted. Of course the landscape will be altered and reconstituted as in almost all of Europe's heritage mining landscapes (some are UNESCO World Heritage Sites). However, people matter too, as do their families. The new mines will sustain an age-old mining community in a region of high unemployment. More importantly, the reopened mines will support the most remarkable Roman mine to be visited in Europe (and with it the later conserved Habsburg village) assuring the Apuseni mountains and Roşia will forever be a focus of tourism during and after the projected gold mining operations.

Finally, let's call a spade a spade: without the mining company the Roman mine of Cătălina Monuleşti will never be maintained by the penniless Romanian state.

Extraordinary archaeology merits vision. Too often it is met with the expectations of unrealistic idealists – dreamers. Look at Italy – world-famous heritage, millions of paying visitors, hopelessly managed archaeological sites falling into disrepair magnificently safeguarded by statutes. At Roşia Montană, a mining company has proposed a realistic solution based upon archaeological research, and at one stroke, the gold mining of Alburnus Maior, with Bucium as one illustration and the underground workings at Roşia Montană as the ultimate excavated experience, could transform Transylvania with its entry-airport at Cluj Napoca, into a Romanist's must-see destination.

Cluj Napoca seems a world away from Roşia Montană and is strangely disinterested in promoting Transylvania. Its name changes illustrate its bid to find its own identity: until recently it was Cluj, gaining Napoca after its Roman ancestry. Before this it was the Hungarian city of Kolozsvar; before that it was one of the seven Saxon fortified cities, Klausenberg (or Clausenberg as it appears in Stoker's novel, *Dracula*). Today a university town of steep, gabled roofs, faded yellow baroque façades and narrow cobblestone streets. Buzzing with bars and cafes, life revolves around the main square dominated by a colossus, a black statue of its greatest son, King Matthias Corvinus, astride a stallion, as well as a glorious gothic cathedral. Traces of the Roman city can be seen beneath a glass panel on one side of the square; much more of its treasures are in store in the city museum, closed indefinitely for restoration, where a forest of monumental tomb inscriptions attest to the Klondyke wealth of the Roman conquerors. Cluj claims that Mozart's *Don Giovanni* was performed here before it was in Budapest, and Liszt certainly loved the town. Without doubt, this vibrant, cultured city has attributes for historical grandeur; the icing on this cake is its proximity to the Apuseni uplands.

I savoured a memorable taste of those rolling hills: roebuck for dinner with a fine Romanian wine in the Plaza Hotel, reflecting upon what an opportunity Romania possesses to take advantage of its Roman past, making it work to bring this seemingly lost region back to life. Dracula, the Pied Piper and Vlad the Impaler made no lasting impact on this blissful land; the Romans did.

Taste

20

Tuscan Cooking Classes and S. Pietro d'Asso

Figure 20 U Penn students excavating the hilltop manor at S. Pietro d'Asso, with Monte Amiata in the distance, 2010.

For years I have directed small armies of excavators through a project manager, so returning to the role of quartermaster (and co-director) was, to be truthful, both nostalgic and scary. I have always said an excavation runs on its food and accommodation. Rather like a well-honed army, fuel up the excavators, create an atmosphere of expectation and fun, and the dig will proceed at a blistering and focused pace. So, when a few days beforehand I learnt that the Tuscan school where we were housing the team lacked showers, I resisted the temptation to panic – I just woke early in a sweat! Fortunately, Montalcino's mayor came up with a solution: we could use the town's main school (and, of course, the students would then add to the polyglot international diversity in this quintessential hilltop town). The kindly mayor awarded us three classrooms and a corridor sufficiently wide for an office. The showers – the apparent bonus – lay a block away in a new sports' hall down the road. One communal shower for the boys; one for the girls … The real bonus in the mayor's largesse, as it happened, were the school cooks. Tuscan schools eat Tuscan food. Imagine it! With litres of red brunello wine served in pitchers thrown in for cultural good measure. The two cooks were exactly what we needed – caring mums who were fascinated by the mix of hungry Italian excavation supervisors, and effervescent American undergraduates. Indeed, by the end of the dig, they were running a cooking class.

The students on seeing their dorms through the prism of jet-lag managed to contain their immediate alarm. Sauntering down the street in only a towel seemed to hold no fears for them (but subsequently they admitted it did). Tuscan food, though, works magic: so, apart from the fare prepared by our two wizards, I took the ensemble to a bar as dawn broke to feast on fresh-baked *cornetti* (of the mouth-melting kind) filled with a choice of cream, *frutta della bosca* or jam, and then, just to make sure that the eager beavers sustained a lively digging pace, each morning I ventured to a grocer's shop to buy kilos of fresh cherries. Was it surprising that after four weeks in this corner of paradise, the team partied and excavated with equal vigour?

Now, of course, a new dig is not only about bed and board. There are the intriguing initial encounters between students and supervisors – in this case Americans (with one Spaniard and one Scotsman) and Italians. With the temperatures soaring to 40 degrees, and the thankless task of topsoil and vegetation removal occupying the first days, I wondered how this cultural encounter might fare. My anxiety was misplaced. The students – three men and eleven women – engaged with an enthusiasm that left me thrilled. They were undeniably shattered by the first three days, but were determined to resist the heat and build a rapport with their bosses. So, the weeks passed swiftly: with the World Cup being soon forgotten as trips to famous places were, in turn, utterly eclipsed by a night festival in a remote hilltop town with swimming in the Mediterranean to follow. Of course, as this was a summer school, due diligence was done to educating the team: my co-directors and I proffered lectures on the project and its significance; the students were attentive and even eager. But truth be told, it was their good humour for each other and the grind of field archaeology in record temperatures that made me nostalgic for those times when I was a supervisor or digger galvanized by the fray of new relationships, too much drinking and the hunt to answer historical questions in truly sublime places.

Truly sublime . . .? Most mornings a lingering mist drifted limply over the lower valleys as we hurtled in a convoy of vehicles from our breakfast bar down the series of hairpin bends to the old Via Cassia. Turning onto a white gravel road we would then go no less quickly parallel to the Asso river, curving up onto a spur before descending down into woodland, and then arriving at an abandoned farmhouse almost encircled by new vineyards. The 10-minute trip was breathtaking whatever time of day. A ballooning dust melted over our vehicles like soft sugary powder, transforming them into phantoms. The farmhouse itself had been deserted only recently. A simple church with the uprights to support a bell, now missing, forms one side, a dark barn lay alongside, then stairs led up to a porch and a great farm-kitchen beyond which were numerous rooms for an ample family. The pigsties looked as though they had been occupied only a winter or two before. Apparently a Romanian had been the last resident; he tended to the miles of vines before the machines were introduced. His material remains were paltry but intriguing: a dictionary and an illustrated schoolbook history of Italy, well-thumbed and discarded on the naked springs of a bed. Had he been taking naturalization exams, whiling away evening hours in this remote but blissful spot, hopeful of becoming an Italian citizen?

Remote San Pietro might be, but at hourly intervals monstrous vehicles passed by. These contraptions blow fine protective powders over the vines, and deal with weeds. Truth be told, these noisy interruptions were soon forgotten, as the eye was drawn daily to the skies over Monte Amiata to the south. Between us and the chestnut woods atop of this extinct volcano lay fields and vines and not, as far as I could see, one dwelling. In our last week, as storms broke the fearsome heat, their arrival was announced first, by wisps of galloping clouds, then tsunami-like cumulus powerfully enveloping all before them. The evening air brings a benediction.

So what did we find? First, a young 90-year old from the neighbouring village told us that the church in the farmhouse was used on the saint's day when he was a boy. The bell, he speculated, was pilfered during the war. He had fought the British in East Africa and he owed his arresting Glaswegian accent to eight years in POW camps in Scotland and Ely. Eight years lost, he lamented. Inside the chapel was an early twentieth-century painting featuring three saintly figures above the simple altar. The lurid colours suggested something from a tourist souvenir shop, but closer inspection revealed that St. Peter stood between the Archangel Michael, and amazingly, St. Conrad II, the eleventh-century German emperor who for a time held sway over much of Italy. Of all the saints, St. Conrad, we asked ourselves? But Conrad reappeared elsewhere to compound our puzzlement.

Originally, we believed the monastery occupied the glorious spur above the farmhouse. Tell-tale potsherds and the excavated remains of a stone tower indicated as much. A magnetometer survey purported to confirm this. But this majestic location was unoccupied save for the tower on its highest knoll which had been constructed on a north–south axis (i.e. at an angle to the Asso river), never finished, then rebuilt on an east–west axis ... and again, it was never finished. This was surely intended to be the *rocca* of the monastery's *borgo*, its projected village. Perhaps the abbot aimed to occupy it and for some reason never did. The sherds show that this flurry of construction led to a foreclosure early in the eleventh century. The one legible coin found was issued by none other than Conrad, the German emperor who 1,000 years later figured in the painting in the chapel below.

So where was the monastery? It was not rocket-science to locate this celebrated house that lasted for 500 years before being eclipsed by its neighbour, Sant'Antimo, in the early thirteenth century. Its west aisle survived to eaves height, reused as a dark manger in the farmhouse. A central nave survived beneath the farmhouse, and the present chapel overlies perhaps the oldest part of the church. Beyond the apses were simple graves. Then, on the flat apron of land in front of the farmhouse, where we parked our cars, half-exposed wall-tops hinted at a hectare of monastic buildings. A magnetometer survey confirmed this. Does this monastery date back to the age of King Aripert, who founded it in *c.* AD 650, according to an eighth-century document? So far, only one eighth-century copper-alloy cloak fastener attests to these beginnings.

Yet the preserved Romanesque monastery is grandiose in design, extraordinarily well-preserved within the bowels of the farm, and definitely holds many secrets.

To conclude, we found the monastery, but not where we expected. Isn't that the real pleasure of archaeology – not knowing? The 'foreclosure' on the hilltop castle is intriguing: what happened to S. Pietro d'Asso in the age of Conrad II? More research is needed and no-one will quibble with that prospect. As for the early Medieval monastery, whose story drew us here, sealed beneath its Romanesque successor, it remains tantalizingly within our future reach! All in all, between the students, the divine tastes of Tuscany, the spirit of the place and the elusive monastery, it proved a memorable month even for an old hand at excavation.

21

Red Mullet and Retsina on Aegina

Figure 21 Aegina: simple ninth-century stone houses, made from recycled Mycenean and Roman material.

Like Lawrence Durrell, I find islands irresistible. I am what he calls a born 'islomane'. Durrell speculates that such people are descendants of the lost city of Atlantis. Of this I am not quite so sure, but the mere knowledge of going to Aegina, whatever growing pains Greece was experiencing, certainly thrilled me. That said, as the aeroplane circled to land at Athens international airport I half expected to see a riot on the runway. The hysteria in the press immediately after the first failed spring election in Greece seemed to be paving the way for the end of the world as we have known it. Six months earlier, I had been in Athens itself to give a lecture in the American School of Classical Studies and, unable to resist the tear gas, had gone past the Parliament and through the streets to the Plaka to take my own sounding on the Greek crisis. On that blissful December day I frankly found little to trouble me until I ran into a squad of riot police, armoured as if for American (NFL) football, having some down time. At the lecture that December night, aside from much chatter about the future of Greece itself, I was advised to visit the excavations on Aegina, where similar mid-Byzantine discoveries to ours made in Butrint, Albania had been recently found. I needed no second invitation, although I was half wondering as the plane rolled into the terminal building if my curiosity was a little imprudent.

Athens airport used to be a by-word for inefficiency. Now it works like clockwork, as did the rental (albeit expensive) of a clapped out little car to take me around Athens to the port of Piraeus. The Saturday traffic was light and, frankly, eagle-eyed for signs of the meltdown, all I could detect was a metropolitan tawdriness to Piraeus which has barely changed since I first ventured here 40 years ago. Gingerly entering Gate E8 (one needs to know this beforehand), a bevy of ferry salesmen alighted upon me with frenzied delirium. Getting a ticket was easy, therefore, and as ever the ferrymen ushered me into the cavernous hold of their ship with a passion that suggested space was at a premium when, in fact, there were only a few other Saturday travellers. In short, the urgency and ritual of the ferry business, it seemed to me as I seated myself on the top deck to take in the Saronic Gulf, was unchanged, crisis or no crisis.

The crossing to Aegina takes a blissful hour. The unedifying clutter of Piraeus is soon forgotten and the glorious marine vistas of an inner sea, hammered blue, reminiscent of the Aegean fill the far horizon. Gone is all sense of metropolitan madness: only the chasing seagulls and their erratic acrobatic displays puncture an otherwise tranquil transition to an island beyond which lie the dark, vertiginous mountains of the southern Peloponnese.

The mission of most visitors to Aegina is the Acropolis-sized temple at Aphaea. But I made the 20-mile crossing to visit the island's main ancient settlement on a low headland jutting into still waters on the northern edge of Aegina town.

Dominated by a tall Doric column resembling an obelisk from afar belonging to the Venetian period (lending its name to the site, Kolona), this is a man-made hill containing a rollercoaster history. First occupied in Neolithic times, this was a major fortified town of the Mycenean period. Its principal Greek building was a temple to Apollo belonging to Aegina's apogee as a trading town before Athens overran it during the bitter Peloponnesian wars. With a seductively safe harbour on this shipping route, such a place was not deserted for long. A Hellenistic trading town was created here; later the entire headland was encircled by powerful late antique fortifications. More interesting still, is a ribbon of mid-Byzantine dwellings tucked under the lea of the hill close to the present foreshore. From the excavations of this miscellany of structures was recently found the rare – rarest – remains of the ninth century, coins and pots. Then the headland, it seems, was abandoned in favour of an inland location secure, so the sources tell us from waterborne terrorism. German archaeologists brought this long saga to light, following in the footsteps of Heinrich Schliemann in search of Homeric warriors, and fascinated by Aegina's place in the larger history of the Saronic Gulf.

The excavations – especially the latest phases – challenge our preconceptions about the past and perhaps the present. More of that in a moment. But first I should continue my travelogue. Ancient Aegina lies within spitting distance of the harbour, so I raced along, parked beside the archaeological site, rushed in at 2.40 . . . and was politely told it closed at 3pm. So goodbye! Crisis or no crisis, British punctuality in this case had long outlasted Bryon's dominant part in the war of independence! Somewhat irked I sought solace in a plate of red mullet and a karafe of retsina as the only diner in a row of quayside restaurants. Here, I read more on the Greek crisis and began to empathize with the impatience of German bankers. Revived, in a good mood, I set off to visit the great temple of Aphaea on the opposite side of the island. I arrived by way of the deserted Medieval hilltop village of Paliachora at 5pm and, would you believe it, like a gaggle of other tourists, I found the massive temple closed for the day.

Undaunted, this forced me back across the island to explore Aegina town. Here, discretely tucked back from the promenade, I discovered the Markopolous Tower, a miniature castle worthy of a Hebridean island, which between 1827 and 1829 apparently served as the first parliament of an independent Greece.

Unheralded as a monument to modern Greece, this was a parliament designed for a miniscule bureaucracy that most European bankers would today applaud.

Next morning I was present at ancient Aegina as it opened and, notwithstanding its four officials, was lucky to have it to myself as they sat and chatted inside the little museum. The museum is a treat: at least for the Neolithic, Mycenean and Hellenistic periods (the Byzantine material, unique though it is, was not deemed worthy of display). The Mycenean finds of jewellery and pottery show that Aegina was undoubtedly one of those places that, in the excavators' minds, must surely have supplied forces to lay siege to (Homer's) Troy. The Mycenean citadel, in essence a palatial block-house, powerfully built and repeatedly refurbished, occupies only the upper contours of this low headland. Commanding the seaways from the south-west towards Athens, this served as a seamark for the sailors of the Saronic Gulf. It is an obvious candidate for Atlantis, largely lost below later iterations of Aegina carefully positioned on this spot. In many ways the formidable Late Antique defences echoed the militaristic sentiments of the Bronze Age architects. Again, this was a powerful bulwark, this time for an empire conscious of its vulnerability as, according to the influential Byzantine *Chronicle of Monemvasia*, refugees found protection here as the mainland was overrun by Slavs. Surely, then, so the thrust of history should lead us to suppose, the Dark Age – ninth-century – successor settlement should have been cocooned within other fortifications, deterrents to interlopers, pirates and every kind of perceived menace as listed in the tersely written Byzantine annals of this epoch? In fact, as at Butrint (in my excavations) where the 840s manor-house belonging to a Byzantine regional official pointedly lies in the old suburb outside the Roman city fortifications, so here too, the well-healed ninth-century community – judging from the scale of the two-storey buildings, their coins and pots – was unfortified. As at Butrint, the buildings themselves are hardly impressive in monumental terms. Most possessed small rooms with first-floor living above and made much use of cut blocks and ashlar taken from earlier phases of this age-old place. Clearly an absence of elegance or grandiosity was not an issue. Ninth-century Aegina was strategically situated on the foreshore to take full advantage of growing maritime commerce between the western Byzantine Empire, especially connecting Malta and Sicily to the southern Balkans and Constantinople.

In an age of infidel Arab and Viking marauders whose staple trade was human trafficking, unfortified places like Aegina and Butrint beg an obvious question. How much can we trust the twitter-laconic contemporary texts? Like the newspapers today were these chronicles written with an agenda? Places like ninth-century Aegina and Butrint clearly prospered from international commerce and were not to face serious threats to their civil society until the later tenth century when urban defence became a standard feature once more and remained an essential ingredient until the nineteenth century. Is there something of a lesson for those reading today's story? Greece, according to the reports, is on its knees, struggling to survive. In the birthplace of the Greek parliament, such hysteria appeared to be plainly exaggerated. That said, a few changes might be welcomed. Reforming the scheduled opening hours of Greece's main assets, its archaeological sites, to fit the programmes of its clients as opposed to following an obtuse law – as Italy has done – might go some way towards redressing a balance of perspective. Being oblivious to the crisis may not have worried the site guards but it scared the waiters in the tavernas.

In the end, of course, places like Aegina will endure, as they always have. As in the paradoxically peaceful ninth century, the pleasures (and produce) of the sea (especially the red mullet) will draw visitors back to enjoy a perspective on the world that is mostly serene and encompasses millennia, not brief turbulent moments.

22

The Taste of Key Lime Pie

Figure 22 The Keys: the overseas railway that became US Route 1.

Archaeology comes in many forms. This much is very evident in the Florida Keys, the pencil-thin chain of 1,000 islands that arcs westwards to its terminus at the southernmost town of the USA, Key West. Ernest Hemingway's Professor Macwalsey in *To Have and Have Not* (1937) calls the Keys 'a strange place, a kind of Gibraltar of America'.

Described as paradise by the natives, conchs (pronounced conks), these shelf-like islands were once covered by an inhospitable mesh of dense mangroves, beggaring belief as to why any pioneer would want to bother to conquer the archipelago. Wintertime is magical (as magical as the eponymous Key lime pie, a melting fantasy of a sweet for the saintly), but come summer, the sub-tropical temperatures are ferocious, when the Keys might just seem closer to desert island hell. But pioneers come in all shapes and sizes, and these islands have had their fair share of them.

First, there were native Indians, principally Calusta vying with the Tequesta tribes, exploiting the abundant marine life, the dolphins, seals, tarpin, lobster and celebrated stone crabs. Fishing here is a breeze, as the flocks of pelicans gliding by demonstrate with effortless ease. At Crane Point, the neatly arranged Natural History Museum (of Marathon) contains a Callusta dug out canoe, shards of their hand-made decorated pots and lithics from Key Marco (in south-west Florida), excavated in 1896 by Smithsonian anthropologist, Frank Cushing. The Callusta came seasonally over the course of two millennia, so it is thought, to escape the infernal mosquitos around their main homelands in south-west Florida. Using sink holes of fresh water, these fishermen apparently defied the conditions, camped on the narrow beaches, and made absolutely no impact upon the mangroves. Caribbean pirates were here too, enjoying not only the fish but also the vulnerable galleons ploughing their way across the Gulf of Mexico. Gold dubloons figure in the Crane Point museum, but the most vivid artifact from this era of lawless seaways is a complete Bellarmine stoneware flask, made in the Rhineland, its rotund belly graced with the coat of arms of Amsterdam. Made to carry sweet Rhenish beer and better known from anchorages around the North Sea, this complete vessel dates to approximately 1565–1585, the age of Queen Elizabeth I. It was scooped, intact, from a deep channel west of Marathon.

Key West owes its origins to nineteenth-century pioneers who recognized its importance as a point of transshipment between Cuba and the new America. Originally owned by the Spanish and called Cayo Hueso, it was bought in 1821 for $2,000 by an American businessman, John Simonton. The low-slung remains of Fort Zachary Taylor, a civil war fortress constructed by the unionist defenders of the town, illustrates the perceived value of this toehold in a maze of mangrove-covered atolls.

One pioneer from this era was George Adderley who, aged 28, having married Olivia, moved from the Bahamas to Marathon to carve out a patch in the mangroves. Earning his living from sponge fishing, and serving as a lay preacher to the few inhabitants of these remote islands, Adderley constructed a simple dwelling set back from what later became Crane Point. The simple bungalow with its four bare rooms and an outside kitchen made of timber remains to this day. This was a tabby house, typical of the Caribbean, the innards of its whitewashed walls constructed of mud and broken seashore boulders melded together using lime made from burning seashells. Adderley House is the essential counterpoint to the grand early twentieth-century houses (like Ernest Hemingway's) that lined the boulevards of the old port of Key West. The palpable hardship invested in this place begs the obvious question of motive. Why did George and Olivia do it, raising a family, and only selling out to the Cranes in the late 1940s? Could they have foreseen the coming of the railway, and the handsome bounty they received for permitting it to beat a path through their own patch of watery jungle? To be fair, for a brief moment, as you encounter Adderley House in the cleared glade on the trail to Crane Point, you could be momentarily in a wood in Surrey. However, the reality of gigantic iguanas thirsting after passing insects soon dispels this fleeting illusion.

The real father of the Keys, the person who confronted the mangroves and shaped its modern guise, was an improbable oil tycoon called Henry Flagler (there is an exhibition dedicated to his memory at Key West's Museum of Art and History (formerly the Old Custom's House)). Flagler was born in 1830, lost a fortune in the civil war, and made an even bigger fortune when he created Standard Oil. The founder of Palm Beach and 'father of Miami', Flagler had a Caesarian ambition that only the extraordinary barons of this 'gilded age' could turn into reality. He invented the Florida East Coast Overseas railway, which took in the 128-mile stretch of the mangrove-covered keys. Key West, being by this time Florida's most populated town, its future looked rosy with the prospective opening of the Panama Canal and a great deal more seaborne traffic between Key West and California. In 1912, one year before Flagler's untimely death, after six years of dare-devil construction, linking island after island, and in one point spanning channels seven miles wide, this monumental feat of engineering was completed. The mangroves had been conquered.

The seven-mile bridge just west of Marathon is the ageless monument to Flagler. Best viewed from the construction-workers' dormitory island, Pigeon Key, the graceful, effortless, parabola of the bridge is worthy of Augustus or a Pharaoh. Flagler's extraordinary railway serviced the Keys until a Force 5 hurricane on Labor Day, 2 September1935. The 17-foot tidal wave ripped long tracts of it apart and in the cataclysmic process killed hundreds of railway men seeking refuge in the lea of its great piers and steel girders. Within three years, the track was reconfigured as the southernmost tract of US 1, the national highway that connects the east coast communities along the 2,369 miles from Key West to Fort Kent, Maine on the Canadian border. Stop off at the Buena Honda State Park, and the staggering ambition of America's pioneers lies before you. The concrete piers are no more than those employed by Roman bridge builders two millennia ago, but above them towers a forest of steel trusses, laced together as firmly as the mangrove plants that were swept away. Flagler's railway was completed here in 1909, collapsed in the 1935 hurricane, and transformed soon afterwards into US 1 (Overseas Highway), which was diverted onto its present alignment in the 1970s. This preserved tract of the highway in the park, is today the place of choice, rather like the Colosseum in Rome, for a smartphone snap. Surrounded by a flat expanse of pewter-grey ocean, it gives a sense, albeit not exactly a correct one, of Flagler's ambitious gilded age railway.

US 1 brought a new kind of tourist and even those, like Francis and Mary Crane, who decided to make their winter homes in the Keys. These were discrete invaders, seduced by the tropical ecology as much as the January sunshine. The most prominent of these Christmas holiday migrants was President Truman, who made his winter White House at Key West and for Christmas dinner had cook-outs instead of turkey and trimmings. Few places could have seemed farther from Washington and anguish about the A-bomb and the Korean War.

Today, the gaudy, hooting motorized conch train around Key West serves the flood of tourists seeking the balmy weather which graces this archipelago. Paradise has moved downmarket to the extent that almost every point where there is width either side of the route 1 highway, the mangroves have been eliminated in place of strip malls. What would pioneers as different as George Adderley and Henry Flagler make of this anonymity? Thanks, though, to the Cranes, the park and museum at Marathon, a tract of the natural Keys survives, as do a host of places where the wild bounty of these linked islands, grouper and yellowfin as well as stone crab, are the main entrees on offer (followed, of course, by Key lime pie). Once tried, never forgotten.

Touch

23

Touching 'Gold' in Gordion

Figure 23 Gordion tumuli on the Anatolian plateau.

When thinking of last summer, one day stands out above all others: my first trip to Gordion (ancient *Gordium*), a Turkish city associated with Midas and the golden touch of a (University of) Penn(sylvannia) professor, Rodney Young. From all I had heard, I assumed it would be arid and charmless. But archaeologists are the very worst travel guides. Seldom, if ever, do they prepare one for the spirit of a place, let alone its defining beauty. Instead, they recall the long months of hardship and the heat. So let me begin by saying that Gordion is extraordinarily and unexpectedly beautiful. Little over one hour by car west of Ankara, you descend a ridge of rolling hills and sweep down towards the site conscious of a great expansive plain reaching perhaps 100 kilometres into the distance. Only faint traces of villages shaded by thin stands of trees tucked away on low promontories punctuate this mesmerizing panorama. This is a big landscape, befitting a lost city with an epic history. Wheeling effortlessly above these grasslands as we drew closer were storks, their magnesium-white wings shimmering in the morning sunshine as they lumbered higher and higher in search of pockets of air.

Today the village of Yasilhöyuk is home to Gordion, 10 kilometres from the burgeoning city of Polatli. Apart from its museum, Yasilhöyuk has a shabby little bar, and appears, like so many Turkish villages, to have been emptied of its citizens who have migrated to the cities where there are schools and the convenience of shopping malls.

Gordion has a great history, hard to imagine where the noise of sheep-bells is the only distraction. Much of this, of course, centred upon the ancient town, a huge mound a mile beyond the village. The mound, though, is only half the archaeological story. Gordion's cemetery of more than 100 earthen tumuli – including the colossal mound MM – is itself a city of Phyrgian dead.

Gordion was the home of Midas, a legendary figure in world history. A Phyrygian king, our first account of Midas comes from the records of his Assyrian neighbour, Sargon between 717 and 709 BC. Midas, it seems, posed a threat to Sargon who first sent diplomats, then an invading force to Phrygia. No war, apparently, ensued. According to the Greek and Roman sources Midas possessed immense wealth. The legend of his golden touch has its origins in a poem by the Spartan, Tyrtaios. Each era was especially fascinated by Midas's death in about 695 BC. Ovid believed that he committed suicide by drinking bull's blood; Plutarch says his suicide was the result of nightmares, and Strabo associated it with the Cimmerian invasion of Phyrgia.

Gordion undoubtedly flourished under the Phyrgians, but this location also attracted major successor towns. A Hellenistic town followed Alexander the Great's triumphal sweep across Anatolia. It was Alexander in 333 BC, according to tradition, who cut (or otherwise unfastened) the celebrated Gordion knot. This intricate knot joined the yoke to the pole of a Phyrgian wagon on the acropolis of the city. Associated with origins of the Phrygian dynasty, it was prophesied that whomever cut the knot was destined to rule Asia. The

Hellenistic town lasted until the Celts arrived in the early third century BC. By 189 BC, apparently, the town was abandoned when the Roman general Manlius Vulso, at the request of the kingdom of Pergamon, marched here. Refounded in the early first century AD as the short-lived Roman colony of *Vindia* or *Vinda*, the town crops up on the Roman itineraries. There were also smaller Later Roman, Selçuk and even Ottoman villages here, and by 1900 when German archaeologists, Gustav and Alfred Körte arrived in search of Midas, a village called Bebi occupied the main mound. Bebi disappeared dramatically in 1921 when the Greek invasion of Anatolia was halted hereabouts in the Battle of Sakarya that brought the victorious Turkish general, Kemal Ataturk to power. The present village of Yasilhöyuk, then, is the last vestige of a community with roots that extend on and off back to Midas and before, to the origins of the Phyrgian dynasty.

Rodney Young from the University of Pennsylvania is synonymous with Gordion. He started excavating here in 1950 and spent twenty-four seasons bringing the ancient place to life again before he died in an accident in 1974. A large, charismatic man, celebrated for his bravery as an ambulance driver during World War II in Greece, Young was fascinated by the Phyrgian story. His legacy has been pursued by his pupils, loyal to his memory, using the camp he built on the edge of the village as a base to process and publish sixty years' worth of research. American classical archaeologists, Kenneth Sams from Chapel Hill and Brian Rose from Penn, are Young's successors as co-directors, while Frank Matero from Penn's Historic Preservation department has charge of conservation as well as making the mound accessible to a new generation intrigued by stories of Midas and this Anatolian archaeology in particular.

Young concentrated upon one section of the mound, revealing metres of deep deposits reaching down to the Bronze Age. The most stunning remains are the immense Phyrgian fortifications of the eighth century BC, now skilfully restored by the Penn team led by Matero. Inside the walls was a grand house with a coloured pebble mosaic, now transferred to the village museum. Like any city of this era, it is a difficult story to grasp from gazing at the wisps of walls, but set in this flat landscape with immense sky, listening to the larks, it is not hard to imagine the impact of Midas, Alexander and the restless Roman military presence here. The mound, though, is only a fraction of the palimpsest of urban remains. New geophysical surveys show that the lower city at one time covered an even larger area; added to that, beyond the cemetery there was countless tumuli.

The mound with its urban story, though, is seldom visited because, as a monument, it has been overshadowed by the great tumulus MM, 165 feet high and covering an area of 55,000 square yards, adjacent to the inviting little site museum in Yasilhöyuk. MM is a Silbury Hill on the Anatolian plateau; a feat worthy of the pyramids, which led to Rodney Young's most sensational archaeological endeavour.

After five seasons at Gordion, Young found the excavation of this earthen pile irresistible. How was he to pinpoint the tomb it contained? He explains as follows: 'The problem was considered from various angles until finally a promising solution was offered by good friends with experience in drilling for oil. A light drilling rig was procured, with which it was possible by a succession of borings to locate and map the area beneath the mound occupied by the pile of loose stones which experience had taught us to expect overlying the tomb chamber. At the same time there was no danger that the drill would go through the stone-pile to do damage within the tomb itself.'

With the strata and configurations of the mound calculated, Young pondered how to enter it. A tunnel was needed. Prudently, Young imported miners from the Zonguldak mining region of Turkey to do the job. 'The miners', Young recorded, 'set a noble example by working around the clock in three shifts'. In 25 days they made a shaft 230 feet long reaching a wall around the buried mausoleum itself. The shaft, refreshingly cool inside, has been kept to allow visitors, as well as the Penn project staff, to gain access to its centerpiece, an extraordinary mortuary house made of timber piles now protected within a great steel cage.

The tomb was intended for a single burial and had no door. Above it was a raft of long logs that covered the roof and served to distribute the immense pressure of the colossal mass of earth and stones of the mound. The great mausoleum, entirely made of fashioned pine logs, measured about 17 by 20 feet and is about 10 feet high. The roof was made of long squared beams, perfectly preserved, supported on shallow triangular gables at the ends and by a comparable gable in the centre.

The dead man had been laid, head towards the east, on a king-size four-poster bed to the north side of the chamber. Elderly and five foot two inches tall, he was initially identified by Young as Midas. However, recent radiocarbon and dendrochronological studies indicate that, in fact, this extraordinary Phyrgian version of a pyramid was the burial place of Midas's father. Around the bed was arranged a wealth of furniture and household items, including three capacious bronze cauldrons. Although not dripping in gold, this treasure, now in the Museum of Anatolian Civilization in Ankara, brings vividly to life the court and grandiosity of the Phyrgian age when its kings dominated the Anatolian plateau and posed a threat to the Assyrians.

Today, the mausoleum of hewn pine logs is arguably the largest timber building of its age surviving anywhere in the world. Its preservation is no less a marvel than the audacious architecture of this burial-place.

There is so much more than can be said about this place. Its history and archaeology are well told in the little site museum in front of mound MM, although the main treasures are in Ankara. Between the breathtaking serenity of the vast landscape, the storks arcing up into the featureless sky, the epic stories of the Phyrgians, Greeks and Romans, and the irrepressible conviction of Rodney Young in making sense of this peerless archaeology, there is the quintessential alchemy of a great place.

My day ended with a birthday party in the whitewashed dig-house. After cocktails, veterans of Rodney Young's era gathered to toast one of their own. Crammed into the first-floor dining room with the windows thrown open, the wine flowed, as did the toasts. Then, as if on cue, a thunderstorm that had steadily meandered from the far dark horizon finally arrived, hailstones battering the roof and bolts of lightning fitfully illuminating the ancient cityscape. 'Rodney Young is amongst us', one of the veterans gleefully declared, staring at the spasms of phosphoric light. He seemed reassured by 'Rodney's' presence because being at this great excavation without him, even 36 years after his death, seemed just plain wrong.

24

In Touch with Rome's Ex-pat Dead: Rome's Non-Catholic Cemetery

Figure 24 The angel of grief in Rome's non-Catholic cemetery.

'To see the sun shining on its bright grass, fresh, when we visited it, with the autumnal dews, and hear the whispering of the wind among the leaves of the trees which have overgrown the tomb of Cestius, and the soil which is stirring in the sun-warm earth, to mark the tombs, mostly of women and young people who were buried there, one might, if one were to die, desire the sleep they seem to sleep.'

(Percy Bysshe Shelley in a letter to Thomas Love Peacock, 1818)

In the shadow of a pyramid, tucked behind the Aurelian Wall, and a stone's throw from the huge amphorae dump at Testaccio, Rome's non-Catholic cemetery has to be one of the most discrete treasures of Rome. When the burial ground was first selected, it lay beyond the periphery of the eighteenth-century town, close to the San Paolo gate leading to Ostia. In those days, Rome was a small town, straddling the Tiber between the Vatican and what is now the *centro storico* gathered around the Pantheon. Cestius's pyramid lay in open countryside, half an hour's walk away.

When there is so much to see in Rome, why bother with a comparatively modern cemetery, a ten-minute taxi ride from the Colosseum? The answer is simple. First and foremost this park, for that is what it is, is arguably the most beautiful in Rome (which is really saying something). Second, it is dizzily stuffed with monumental archaeology, cared for with a sensitive touch that, let's say, is not exactly the norm in the rest of Rome. Best known as the final resting place of the English romantic poets, Keats and Shelley, it is evident that their hallowed names have drawn about 4,000 other foreigners whose biographies are interwoven into the fabric of modern Rome. In truth, thoughtfully defended, this is Rupert Brooke's far field, for Americans, Britons, Danes, Germans, Swedes and many more besides who fell in love with the eternal city and made it their home.

It is easy to find, of course. One street into the walled city from the pyramid, the cemetery really comprises two parts: the original field first used by exiled members of the Stuart court as well as Grand Tourists in about 1716, and the larger, ordered ranks of monuments shaded by rows of cypresses and pines made after 1822. The two could not be more different. The original field is dotted with graves in no real order, except for the cluster by the far cemetery wall. Otherwise this lightly shaded ground feels like an English city park improbably dominated by Cestius's vaunting cenotaph. Presently, the pyramid is not at its best: it is partly covered with scaffolding where zealous conservators attempt to defrock it of the pollution since it was last cleaned for the millennial celebrations of 2000. Between it and the cemetery lies a sunken enclosure, a sanctuary for well-fed moggies that languidly patrol the cemetery.

In the far corner lies John Keats. Next to him is interred his faithful friend, Joseph Severn, who outlived the poet by 58 years. The graves are simple, worthy of an English churchyard. Nearby, a plaque bearing a medallion portrait of the poet copied from Benjamin Haydon's life mask is inscribed with an elegiac doggerel by a retired army general, Sir Vincent Eyre. Worthy of a barrow-digging poet, the painful rhyme reminds the visitor of Keats's mythic place in Victorian England:

> Keats! If thy cherished name be 'writ in water'
> Each drop has fallen from some mourner's cheek;
> A sacred tribute such as heroes seek,
> Though oft in vain-for dazzling deeds of slaughter
> Sleep on! Not honoured less for Epitaph so meek!

More intriguingly, another memento is inscribed on the reverse of Severn's headstone. Emulating the long tributary lists in English museums of the time, here registered are the establishment figures who subscribed to his tomb. Among them are Longfellow, Millais and Rossetti.

The 'new cemetery' created in stages after 1822 is jam-packed with rows of tombs. Scarcely an inch is spared, giving the visitor a dazzling sense of a Rome *Who's Who*. Extraordinary tombs, simple tombs, mere plaques and posies of wild flowers are jumbled together. Archaeologists rub shoulders with poets, and politicians rub up against architects. The commonality is classical: ancient chests, sarcophagi, columns and half-columns are the prevailing idioms of death. Then, there are sculptures that resonate with archaic Greece and Imperial Rome, tenderly signalling to the living the character of their loss. Several examples of the Roman sarcophagus of Scipio Barbatus, now in the Vatican, are dotted around the graveyard. The most memorable sculpture, though, belongs to the age of the pre-Raphaelites, William Wetmore Story's memorial to his wife, the *Angel of Grief* (1894) in the uppermost part of the cemetery. Achingly poignant, its gossamer fineness cries out to be touched. No less affecting are the unembellished memorials, such as that to the Italian Marxist philosopher, Antonio Gramsci, towards the far end of the graveyard. Pause too, close to Shelley's grave, to pay homage to the English actress Belinda Lee who died in a car crash in California in 1961 following a publicized romance with a Roman prince.

Reflect upon the extraordinary Americans, the Egyptologist philanthropist, David Randall-MacIver – a Monuments' Man who long before left Oxford to be a curator at the Penn Museum; the architect of New York's gilded age,

William Rutherford Mead, one of the celebrity designers of the American Academy of Rome; and an elaborate cenotaph, still regularly tended with posies, to a southern gentleman, Thomas Jefferson Page, who sought exile after bitter defeat in the American Civil War.

This is a place stirred by shafts of sun where the desire to sleep serenely persists nearly two centuries after Shelley commented upon the cemetery that was soon to host his own ashes. Reflect, though, before you leave on how this extraordinary 'park' still operates as an active graveyard. By any archaeological standards it is a curatorial challenge. Some 4,000 monuments erected over the last 300 years nestle below a copse of tall trees fighting to reach above the shadow of the Aurelian Wall. Nevertheless, the cemetery is immaculately maintained, and has the hallmark of any counterpart in Denmark, England or the United States.

This private cemetery is immaculately maintained to a standard which the present Director, Amanda Thursfield, and volunteers like Nicholas Stanley-Price (the author of a marvellous new guide to the cemetery) can rightly take pride. On the one hand, it is regulated to national and city regulations; on the other hand, managed by a small team, admirably aided by volunteers (docents) who answer to an unpaid board of ambassadors. The trees pose a tough challenge. Before they fall prey to heavy winds or age, and tumble onto graves, they must be monitored and removed. Expensive and complicated though it is to pluck an ageing umbrella pine from the dense serried ranks of tombs, there is no choice but to act. Like a bad tooth, with a crane that can extend its reach over the Aurelian Wall, the ailing tree must be patiently extracted. Likewise, each tomb, like Cestius's pyramid, has to weather the pollution of this bustling city. Each has been carefully tended and curated for the future. There is an inherent cost, of course, that is not met by revenue from the 20,000 or more visitors each year that seek out this historic oasis. Nevertheless, like the tended grass and the evocatively unkempt wild flowers, there is the pervasive assurance of a sensitive hand at work here. Balancing the books from fees for the plots as well as donations takes real skill. No less skill is required to sustain the serenity of this place as well as its extraordinary encyclopaedic archaeology.

In this cemetery, people matter. Leave it, and in an instant, cluttered around the great pyramid, you immediately sense the inadequacies of Rome's anachronistic antiquities service. Better, perhaps, to amble 300 yards towards the artificial amphora mound of Testaccio, and take lunch in Flavio al Velavevodetto (Via di Monte Testaccio), a restaurant burrowed into the sherds. The menu is both modern and old: traditional dishes associated with the abattoir that was once here, fashioned to contemporary taste. Like the cemetery, it is a pointer to good management, caressing the senses appropriately in this eternal city.

Do buy Nicholas Stanley-Price, *The Non-Catholic Cemetery in Rome. It's history, its people and its survival for 300 years* (Rome 2014), €18. The proceeds of this marvellous new book go towards the upkeep of the cemetery (see www. cemeteryrome.it).

25

Bunga Bunga?

Figure 25 'The bikini girls': fourth-century female athletes of Piazza Armerina (courtesy Patrizio Pensabene).

Apparently *Bunga bunga* loosely describes the energetic antics of courtesans of an Italian Prime Minister! The coarse colloquialism is now also synonymous with the perceived fiscal failings of contemporary Italy, so it is perhaps no surprise that a mosaic in the Late Roman Villa del Casale at Piazza Armerina showing women in bikinis is sometimes taken to mark the beginnings of an apparently infinite age (in the minds of many Italians, at least) of moral decline and fall! Until recently, a sign in this UNESCO World Heritage Site apparently urged visitors to hasten to feast their eyes on these shameless hussies filling a dark room off the Hall of the Great Hunt. In fact, these graceful ladies were preparing for serious games; one blonde is preparing to hurl a discus. The perspective and coloured plasticity of the mosaicist's art is so sensual you long to touch her. Such, however, used to be the asphyxiating heat trapped beneath the old plastic glass covering these precious mosaics that making it along the walkways as far as the bikini girls necessitated the stamina of a serially re-elected septuagenarian Italian Prime Minister. Bikinis seemed appropriate attire in the clawing greenhouse conditions – all but justifying the pragmatic purpose of the old sign!

The Villa del Casale at Piazza Armerina, however, is now no longer a hothouse. Much of it has been gracefully re-covered with a new roof designed by the Milanese conservation architect, Gionita Rizzi, who encouraged me to see and comment upon it. (His portfolio includes covers at the great Mayan capital of Copán in Honduras and Herculaneum, the smaller of the buried Vesuvian cities.) Deep in the building, the air is now cool and, as a result, there is time (or rather the will) to admire these trim athletes for what they are as well as the remarkable ensemble of other narrative floors that surround them.

Located in the centre of Sicily in a deep valley on the western side of the modern town of Piazza Armerina (the so-called 'city of mosaics'), this place possesses an Arcadian beauty. Four hundred thousand visitors a year make this pilgrimage to see the mosaics, mostly in the spring and autumnal months because the legend of the hothouse cover erected in the 1950s is well known. Around the villa, a shanty town of kiosks has evolved, selling souvenirs, some as old as the perspex cover itself. New wooden kiosks have been inserted into the zone between the expansive car-park and the archaeological site, doubling the vending opportunities. So, this villa, with its €10 entrance fee is generating upwards of €5 million a year, a sustainable income that is likely to continue until someone discovers a better villa to market. Hence, the need for the new roof: with more clement conditions, surely more tourists would journey to this secret valley in central Sicily?

For doubters, because the funds ran out, two old parts of the villa have not been re-roofed: the bath-house at the entrance and the separate tricoran reception room. In both, even before the sun is really up, the air is heavy and ferocious sunlight casts shapeless disfiguring shadows over the pavements.

The new roof has been accompanied by two unexpected initiatives: brazen advertising for a nearby outlet shop, and 'an exhibition' (for that is what it is) of zany bronze sculptures and underwhelming installations. But it is the new roof and the (uniformly filtered) light that it throws on the floor-narrative of the villa it covers that have drawn me here on a summer morning.

The villa covers three great terraces at the foot of a steep hill. Unusually for a Roman villa it is arranged in three different axes. On the east side lies the first terrace bounded by an aqueduct, containing private apartments, the grandiose basilica with its marble floor, and the celebrated Hall of the so-called Great Hunt. The second terrace is occupied by the peristyle courtyard and the dining room (triclinium) complex. The monumental tripled-arched entrance to this palatial villa and the suites of baths occupy the first terrace. This compact, yet massive, structure was built on top of an earlier first- to-third-century villa at some time – though no-one, amazingly, knows exactly when – during the mid-fourth century.

The earlier roof, designed by architect Franco Minissi in the 1950s, invoked a science fiction response to great archaeology. It consisted of a lightweight metal skeleton sheathed with plastic, and ventilated by small latched windows rather than the air conditioning the architect had anticipated. Minissi's roof replaced a small, prosaic wooden version over the three-apsed hall covered with clay tiles supported on massive brick pillars. Built by architect Piero Grazzola in the 1940s it had been likened to a hayloft. By contrast, Minissi's design aimed to convey the volume of the rooms containing the mosaics with wall-walks that permitted visitors to see the pavements. The greenhouse effect, however, promoted irregular cycles of expansion and contraction that put the mosaics at risk. Meanwhile the wall-walks were tight passages that required elbowing one's way, somewhat erratically, through the ensemble of buildings, offering little sense of how the villa once functioned as a great house. For its time, though, Minissi's design was a huge achievement, doing much to protect the mosaics as well as to secure them worldwide fame. That said, the translucent cover did not conjure up a palace, except perhaps on the moon.

The great achievement of Rizzi's new cover is simple: the main house with its labyrinth of rooms arranged around the large courtyard feels like the home of a grandee with a voracious appetite for the visual myths and wonders of the then-known world. Whether he was an Emperor or simply a wealthy Mafioso, the galleries of extraordinary mosaics made for him, like magic, now make sense. The elegantly moulded apsed rooms with roofs supported on exposed beams have been cleverly recreated. The exposed aluminium uprights still need cladding and apparently the columns and capitals were to be reproduced in wood following the techniques used in stage set decoration to make sense of the classical articulation of the interiors. But these are details. This renewal is not some tawdry casino-like copy worthy of Las Vegas. The chief excitement generated by the new cover is the plain and simple fact that blazing sunlight no longer makes the mosaics invisible.

The bikini girls, as a result, could not be more seductive. Like all the mosaics here, the detail and colouring are cleverly explicit, the work, many art historians believe, of North African craftsmen. Cleanly lit, it is not so much the artisanal expertise that delights as the intersection of mythical and contemporary stories arranged to enhance the design of the house. Like a great English country house, the imagery has an overarching cohesion. Positioned beyond the long Hall of the Great Hunt, the bikini girls are being put through their paces opposite the ante-chamber to the master bedroom, close to the great reception hall. Perhaps some discrete mischief was being invoked after all? In the cool balmy air created by this re-roofing, you, the visitor, in touch with the vaunting narrative can now judge!

Just as clear, too, are tiny sections of the first rather unappealing geometric mosaics that graced the great house. Who built Piazza Armerina and who then furnished it with the celebrated narrative pavements, pleasingly remains a debate between archaeologists and art historians, as the original excavations were rather impetuously made and failed to check the associated ceramics which might today be precisely dated to a historical personality. Spanning perhaps no more than two or three generations pivoted around the central and later decades of the fourth century, this place has an elegiac whiff of end of empire as its owner in the Great Hall of the Hunt with scenes of Africa and India, plainly attempted to position himself at the centre of the then world.

One other aspect of this new project is obvious. Guards are absent! The elevated walkways, monitored presumably by cameras, make the intrusion of bored and disgruntled attendants superfluous. This ancient country house is now simply filled with people quietly gazing at the floors as though it were an air-conditioned art gallery. The peer-visitor experience is deeply satisfying.

Beyond the villa's monumental entrance I found some draping sun-bleached plastic fences an irresistible invitation: beyond, under makeshift covers, lay the remains of Patrizio Pensabene's recent excavations of the Norman (Medieval) phases of the palace that have yet to be presented to the public. Plainly, after five centuries of abandonment, this mythic place became a palace again for first the Arab and then the Norman conquerors of Sicily. Such a rich story is yet to be told, inviting yet more covers.

Driving back across the burnt sierras to reach the balmy breezes of the coast, musing the glorious enigmas associated with the making of this great country house, I thought what wonderful changes Gionata Rizzi had wrought to the presentation of this world heritage site. So finding a convenient signal on my phone as I awaited sea bass at a maritime *osteria*, I sent him an e-mail venturing my compliments. He replied, almost surprised by my admiration:

> 'What makes me sorry, apart from the unfinished portions, due of course to the fact that we ran out of money (only one small room on the left side of the three-apses triclinium is meant to retain the old shelter as a memory of a project that has been – for better or worse – a milestone of archaeological conservation) is the unfinished inside. Let's hope that, with new finance, this can be accomplished.'

Let's hope Italy finds the finance. After all, the greatest house of the fourth-century world is now, at last, the treat for summer visitors that earlier architects aimed to achieve.

Index